HOWARD VANDERWELL

devotional reflections
Living
and Loving
Life

FAITH
ALIVE®
Christian Resources

Grand Rapids, Michigan

ACKNOWLEDGMENTS

Unless otherwise indicated, Scripture quotations in this publication are from the HOLY BIBLE, TODAY'S NEW INTERNATIONAL VERSION, © 2001, 2005, International Bible Society. All rights reserved worldwide.

Living and Loving Life: Devotional Reflections, © 2010 Faith Alive Christian Resources, Grand Rapids, Michigan.

Printed in the United States of America.

We welcome your comments. Call us at 1.800.333.8300 or email us at editors@faithaliveresources.org.

Library of Congress Cataloging-in-Publication Data
    Vanderwell, Howard.
    Living and loving life : devotional reflections / Howard Vanderwell.
      p. cm.
    ISBN 978-1-59255-568-0
    1. Devotional literature, American. I. Title.
    BV4832.3.V36 2010
    242--dc22

                                       2010045681

10 9 8 7 6 5 4 3 2 1

Contents

Introduction

I am living. And I am loving it.

When I say that I am living, I don't just mean that my physical body continues to function: that my brain waves show activity, my heart keeps pumping blood, and my lungs continue to process oxygen. Oh, that's certainly part of it, because there was a time—actually three times—when disease invaded my body and I wondered if I'd still be alive on this date.

There's so much more to living than just being alive. I've known scores of people—even Christians—who only seem to be existing. They have no spark, no sense of adventure, no eagerness for each day. They have no big dreams to shoot for, no big goals to work toward, no passions to motivate them, no sense of adventure that makes them want to tackle some big challenges.

They may be existing, but they're not living.

I believe God intends much more for us. God created us to live with a healthy sense of purpose and adventure. He built it right into our psychic DNA. When God created Adam and Eve (and us) in his image, he designed us for a span of days and nights and months and years that would include quality involvements, productive purposes, and a sense of privilege. God intended us to be partners in his work in this world. From the time God knit us together in our mother's womb, the psalmist says, "all the days ordained for [us]" were written in God's book (Psalm 139). Before we were born God was already building the need for good living into our very nature. Anything less diminishes the image of God in us.

Being redeemed in Christ raises our calling to an even higher level. It's hard to imagine God's willingness to give up his only Son for a cruel death on planet Earth, and even harder to imagine Jesus' willingness to experience death for our salvation. But I know God's ultimate purpose. Christ came "that [we] may have life, and have it to the full" (John 10:10). Now we're new creatures, pardoned of our guilt, brought into an eternal kingdom, and called to serve God in all we do. That's real living! I'm pretty sure Christ didn't make us into new creatures just to have us fiddle the rest of our lives away.

I've discovered that it's possible to learn more about living the more we live. By now I've passed through most of life's chapters and seasons. I've had the fun of being a child and learning new things every day. I've felt the tension of an adolescent working through the struggles of discovering who I am. I've been a young man who married and learned to face life's challenges together with my wife. I've been a young father delighting in seeing three sons grow from tiny babes to grown men. I've been a middle-aged parent who watched those sons make their commitment to the Lord, embrace the young women who would become their wives, and select the profession that would require all their efforts. Now I'm a grandfather of ten who watches all of them carefully, noticing in their lives some of the same patterns, same characteristics, same struggles I had.

I've been a pastor for all my working life. Even though I'm "retired" now, that's still my identity. I'll always be a pastor. A pastor has the astounding privilege of taking a front-row seat at the drama of what God is doing in people's lives. As a pastor I've worshiped with God's people week after week, year after year. I've celebrated baptisms. I've taught children, answered questions, listened to fears, and watched some fail. I've married people, counseled them, watched their families grow, and buried them. I've wept with them, laughed with them, prayed with them, and played with them. I've brought God's Word to them for their salvation, encouragement, nurture, and correction. I've broken bread and poured out juice with them. And every Sunday I've had the privilege of pronouncing God's benediction on them as they go out to continue living their faith all week.

Through all the seasons of my life and my front-row seat in so many other lives, I've seen a lot of living—good living and not-so-good living, wise living and not-so-wise living. I've seen God faithfully caring for his people, loving them, calling them, growing them, waiting for them, comforting them, and challenging them.

I've also discovered that it's possible to learn a lot about living when you fear that you are about to lose your life.

I faced that possibility first in 1972, just a few months after moving to a new pastorate in Lansing, Illinois. During a routine physical examination, my doctor spoke the words that changed my life: "I don't like what I feel in there." He sent me to a specialist who examined me even more carefully, scheduled me for surgery, conducted a battery of tests, and finally rendered the verdict that it was cancer—Non-Hodgkin's lymphoma. I had just turned thirty-five years old and was the father of three young sons. It felt like someone had levied a death sentence on me. The next three months involved surgery, continual testing, and radiation therapy. Before too long, I had returned to full strength and resumed all my activities. But I was shaken. There in Room 725 at Rush Presbyterian St. Luke Medical Center in Chicago I first faced my mortality: "I could die from this!" And suddenly my life took on a whole new meaning. It was worth fighting for.

From then on, my schedule included regular physical examinations every few months—until 1984, when I discovered another lump. All the old fears welled up again. By then I had moved to Hudsonville, Michigan, my fourth pastorate. More tests, more waiting, more anxiety, more surgery. More cancer, this time Hodgkin's lymphoma. Fortunately the cancer had not spread to other lymph nodes or organs. Total abdominal radiation was the prescribed form of treatment. That represented only one level of pain. The higher and deeper level was the pain of anxiety, fear, and wondering what a second recurrence of cancer would mean for the future.

Then, just six years after the second encounter, a "routine" examination resulted in a doctor saying once again, "I don't like what I feel in there." More specialists, more surgery, more tests, more radiation therapy.

Three times in eighteen years, two different kinds of lymphoma. I have now lived for more than double my age when the first attack occurred. I am now in excellent health—and have been cancer free for nearly twenty years.

I dare say I have lived more in the last twenty years than most people live in their whole lifetime. I'm still a husband, a father, a grandfather, a pastor, a friend, and a child of God. But my life has been richer, deeper, and much more of an adventure than I ever thought it could be. More than ever I love living. I know the day will come when God will ask me to lay it down and come to glory with him, but until that day I am loving living.

During my second encounter with cancer, I wrote a devotional booklet called *Proven Promises*. I wrote it for and to myself as a form of personal devotions. I wrote it candidly and honestly out of the emotions and struggles that major disease involves. I wrote it partly in reaction to much of the literature I had encountered, which seemed far too superficial to me. Others who were suffering found these devotionals encouraging, and they were distributed far and wide, giving me the opportunity to come alongside others facing the same battle I had encountered.

In 2002, I retired from the pastorate but with the growing conviction that God had rescued me those three times so I could continue to serve him. I am now a staff member of the Calvin Institute of Christian Worship at Calvin College and of Calvin Theological Seminary. In both capacities I have the privilege of serving the church, staff members in congregations, and people who are preparing for the Christian ministry by providing counsel and producing materials in the area of worship. I pray that I may satisfactorily fulfill God's intentions to use me for the sake of his church.

This book represents my further reflections on how precious living is and how to make the most of it since *Proven Promises* was written more than two decades ago. I hope you'll think of these devotionals as extended pastoral conversations in which we open our hearts to each other as we search for the richest and most satisfying ways in which to use the years God graciously and providentially gives us.

I'm living and loving it. This book is designed to pass on to you some of that love for living.

Suggestions
for Using These Materials

This book is organized around eight major themes—each with a brief introduction and ten devotionals on each theme. I hope they will stir your own reflections. Here are some suggestions for using these materials:

- Read a devotional each day and enter a time of reflection on your own experiences.
- Write some of your thoughts and reflections on the same theme. Consider using a notebook or your computer to journal your own reflections.
- At the end of each meditation you will find three related Scripture passages (Reflecting on God's Word) for further reading. Decide whether you'd like to read all three on the same day or select one each day to read for further reflection. As you read each passage, add your own reflections in your journal.
- You'll also find questions and suggestions that will aid your personal reflection (For Further Reflection). You can use these for personal reflection or as the basis of discussion with your spouse, family, or a small group. An accountability group with friends would be an excellent setting to reflect on such matters.

As you read and reflect on the themes in this book, may God feed your spirit and deepen your love for life. Above all, may you "grow in the grace and knowledge of our Lord and Savior Jesus Christ" (2 Peter 3:18).

Heart Health

I went to my doctor the other day—again. There are stages in life when we seem to go to doctors more often.

Some of those visits are problem-oriented—something doesn't seem right so you want that checked out. Other visits are "check-ups." There's no identifiable problem, you're just getting a general exam. I'm a firm believer in annual check-ups because two of my occurrences of cancer were detected in routine physical exams. I had no symptoms at all.

Usually I go home from such exams with a sense of relief, happy to have been pronounced "healthy for my age" by the doctor. At the same time, I can't help feeling that the exam has been very incomplete.

The only things my doctor considers are the things he can learn from poking and probing and listening; only the things that can be measured by blood tests and urine tests and x-rays. But I'm so much more than a blob of functioning physical mass. It makes sense to me that some prefer to use the term *wellness*, which encompasses far more than *health*.

I know people whose bodies are functioning very well but I don't consider them healthy at all. I know others whose bodies are not doing so well but—in spite of that—they are living well.

Health is so much more than the physical state of the body.

Good health involves our attitudes, our faith, our values, our goals, and our purpose in life. People who are healthy have embraced a renewing rhythm in life. For them life is more than what can be measured by the clock or the calendar; it's more than the results of blood tests or x-rays.

So let's spend some time in the coming days thinking about our heart health. If you are willing to be honest with yourself, you might just be ready to give yourself the best exam you've ever had.

1. Healed and Whole

I f I allow myself to stop and think about it, the threats that surround me every day are pretty frightening.

I read recently that we have more bacteria on our body than there are people in the United States. Really. Apparently there are 229,000 germs per square inch on frequently used faucet handles, 21,000 germs per square inch on work desks, and 1,500 on each square centimeter of our hands. What's more, the workplace (where I'm writing this) is the worst hiding place for such germs. If you're feeling a little queasy right now, I don't blame you. It's a wonder any of us escape the deadly diseases that are just waiting to strike. It's a wonder any of us are able to function.

And as if that's not enough, think about the miles we drive daily, each trip with the potential of accidents. Think about the temptations that have their hooks in you, the deadly desires of your fallen heart.

All of which leads me to believe that good health is a daily miracle. Let's call it the miracle we all take for granted.

I can make a list of the major diseases from which I've been cured. But I can't begin to remember and number all those that didn't seem so big: everything from ear infections as an infant to last month's encounter with the flu. How about you? Some of the healing we experience takes place through the natural protective functions of our bodies, some with the help of medications or other focused medical care. But all of those healings were given by God.

No wonder David describes God as the one who "heals all [our] diseases" (Psalm 103:3).

In Proverbs, the book of wisdom, Solomon counsels his son with these words: "Do not be wise in your own eyes; fear the LORD and shun evil. This will bring health to your body and nourishment to your bones" (Proverbs 3:7-8).

Is God really that interested in our total health? And does God refuse to draw as sharp a line as we do between our physical health and all the other dimensions of health—emotional, mental, spiritual, and relational? Does he make a direct connection between wisdom, humility, fear, and health? If so, then medical attention is only one part of our wellness program.

Perhaps we make a serious mistake when we think that most of our healing comes through medical attention.

Perhaps, instead, I am whole

- when I am humble before God and not wise in my own eyes.
- when I live with a holy fear of the Lord.
- when I have found a purpose for living that matches God's plan for me.
- when I discern right from wrong.
- when I serve others.
- when my relationships with others are marked by grace.
- when I am filled with the power of Christ's resurrection.
- when I live with the clear conviction that my life counts.
- when . . .

Go ahead—you add to the list!

Reflecting on God's Word

Deuteronomy 5:25-33
Isaiah 58:6-12
Luke 7:18-23

For Further Reflection

1. What is the shape and character of the total health that Christ has made possible for you as a redeemed person? Write some of your thoughts down in your journal.

2. In what ways have you experienced healing from the hand of God in recent years? It may be easy to forget these as time moves on. Recall them and thank God for them.

3. What is the greatest obstacle to your personal wellness at this point in your life? Identify it and ask for God's help in resolving it.

2. Living Water

One day Jesus created quite a stir in the temple in Jerusalem. He told the people who were milling around, "Let anyone who is thirsty come to me and drink. Whoever believes in me . . . rivers of living water will flow from within them" (John 7:37).

The leaders, of course, wanted to arrest him because this sounded like he was claiming to be God. John quickly goes on to explain that Jesus was talking about the Holy Spirit who would be coming soon, as soon as Jesus ascended to heaven.

These are hard words for me to understand. That's because I live in Michigan, the land of rivers, streams, little lakes, big lakes, Great Lakes, and huge underground resources of good water. Michigan is a very special place in North America that has a virtually unlimited supply of fresh water. We turn on the faucet and it flows in abundance. We boat on it, swim in it, irrigate our crops with it, water our lawns with it, and wash our cars with it. We are never thirsty, and we never give a thought to the possibility of all that water ever drying out. It's hard for us to relate to people who get so thirsty that they think they will die or people who live in fear of disease floating in whatever little water they can find.

In a sense, that limits our understanding of what Jesus is teaching here.

He's telling us that healthy and whole living comes when the living water of the Holy Spirit flows freely through your life. No Spirit, no health. That's his point.

Too bad we debate and argue about the Holy Spirit so much. Does he give *these* gifts or *those* gifts? Does he provide all the gifts today, or only some? Is the Spirit's work spectacular or quietly fruitful? Do we sense the Spirit's presence in our assurance of salvation or by having a testimony? Have we all received the Spirit?

Many of us assume the Holy Spirit is like the sort of inoculation you get as a child. Usually you only have to get inoculated once— once vaccinated, always protected. Does the Holy Spirit work that way—once the Spirit's in you, it's like the safety of a permanent in-oculation?

Instead, the Bible teaches that our life with the Spirit is dynamic—ever changing. Some days these "rivers of living water" flow freely, other days they're pretty dammed up. Some days a torrent, other days a trickle.

Why is that?

Paul says that we are "marked . . . with a seal, the promised Holy Spirit" (Ephesians 1:13). But the rest of the New Testament teaches that different types of relationships with the Holy Spirit are possi-ble.

The Bible calls us to "be filled with the Spirit" (Ephesians 5:18). That's when the river of waters flows freely. But sometimes God's people "grieve the Holy Spirit of God" (Ephesians 4:30). At times we "put out the Spirit's fire" (1 Thessalonians 5:19) and "resist the Holy Spirit" (Acts 7:51). In such cases, the river is dammed up—not much more than a trickle can get through.

When it comes down to it, our health and wellness are deter-mined by how well the river flows. And how well the river flows is determined by what we're doing that might obstruct the flow.

Reflecting on God's Word

John 16:5-16

Acts 2:1-4

Ephesians 4:25-34

For Further Reflection

1. Recall a time in your life when you were deeply thirsty spiritually. What caused it? What helped you?

2. Read 1 Corinthians 12:3. In what ways have you professed, "Je-sus is Lord"? What does that say about your relationship with the Holy Spirit?

3. Can you identify ways in which you have "grieved" the Holy Spirit or "put out his fire"? What might that be?

3. Servants

I find it helpful to think of life as a "package" that we receive from our Maker. Even after we open the package, though, none of us knows for sure how many years are included in our life. I've often wondered about mine. At thirty-five years old, I thought I was coming to the end of my life, but now I've more than doubled those years! Life expectancy tables can tell us something, but they deal only with probabilities. Some folks live much longer than expected, others much shorter. None of us can bank on those statistics.

What's more, none of us can control how many years we have. Even if we do the things we should to increase the probability of a long and healthy life—eat healthy foods, nurture loving relationships, and get plenty of rest and exercise—there's no guarantee. So have a lot of other folks whose package contains far fewer years than they'd hoped.

I guess the real question isn't "How many years?" but "What for?"

I'm acutely aware that someday I'm going to have to hand the package of my life back to my Maker. The question at that time isn't going to be "How many days were there?" but "What good were they?" Or "How successfully did you use them in valuable ways?"

What kinds of things will other people say about you when you hand your package back to the Maker? How will your children or other people who knew you well remember you? What will they say about how you've used your time?

This isn't just some end-of-life check-up. My view of what life is for affects what I do today and what I plan for tomorrow. It shapes what I consider valuable and how I use my time.

I'm sometimes haunted by the people I've encountered for whom daily living can best be described as cold mashed potatoes or Pepsi that's lost all its fizz. They seem to live with few goals and even less personal satisfaction. I fear how they will react when they hand the package back and have nothing to show for it.

The apostle Paul's passion for living is no secret. Here's a man whose satisfaction seems to grow as he nears the end of his life.

Here's a man who can talk about knowing a crown of righteousness is in store for him when that day of handing back the package finally comes (see 2 Timothy 4:7-8). What does that take? What kind of people can have that kind of confidence?

Jesus set the standard for us in his own ministry. "Whoever wants to become great among you must be your servant," he said, "and whoever wants to be first must be slave of all. For even the Son of Man did not come to be served, but to serve, and to give his life as a ransom for many" (Mark 10:43-45).

That's it. That says it all. Once you say "serve," not much more needs to be said.

Notice that Jesus sets his own ministry as the pattern we're supposed to follow. You can capture his whole motive for coming to earth in the single word *serve*. There is only one way to explain Jesus' willingness to give his life as a ransom, and it's found in that word. It means intentionally looking for ways to do what the master wants done.

Imagine handing that package back, no matter how many years it has contained, and seeing that the package is wrapped in a cover with the word *servant* written boldly over it!

Reflecting on God's Word

Proverbs 3:5-6
Matthew 20:20-28
John 13:1-17

For Further Reflection

1. Write down a brief statement you'd like others to be able to include as an epitaph on your gravestone.

2. Search for some way today in which you can extend a deliberate act of service to someone in need. After you have done it, reflect on how it affected the person you served—and how it affected you.

3. Identify someone you know quite well whom you would describe as a "servant." Write down in your journal what it is about that person that you most admire.

4. Compassion

Healthy people are compassionate people. Compassionate people are healthy.

It goes both ways.

But I find it both hard and easy to be compassionate.

Let's take the "easy" side first. After all, I have experienced the richest compassion there is, straight from heaven through the heart of Christ to me. It has given me a new life—freedom from my sins, the hope of eternal life, the constant companionship of Christ in my daily walk, and big purposes for living. There's no greater compassion than that. Having experienced compassion in such rich measure, shouldn't it be the easiest thing in the world to show to others? As John says, "since God so loved us, we also ought to love one another" (1 John 4:11).

Jesus' whole life and ministry is a perpetual parade of compassion. Matthew tells us that Jesus traveled through all the towns in Palestine, where people were hungry to hear the good news and eager to be healed of all kinds of diseases. And when Jesus saw the crowds, "he had compassion on them, because they were harassed and helpless, like sheep without a shepherd" (Matthew 9:36).

Every time I read that verse, I recall a story about a group of children who were standing in a huddle on the playground, most of them crying. In the center was a young boy doubled over in pain. The teacher approached the group and asked what the problem was. One little girl answered, "We've all got a pain in Jimmy's stomach."

That's the best definition of compassion I've ever found. It's the ability to feel someone else's pain in my stomach. Those who have been loved by Christ ought to have sensitive stomachs. It's part of being healthy.

Those who are members of a healthy Christian congregation have experienced compassion there too. When needs come up, there are always people who care. They'll ask about your welfare, pray for you, bring in meals, and help in a variety of ways. The community of faith is a good place to be when you are in need.

At the same time, showing compassion sometimes feels like the hardest thing to do. We're naturally selfish, and we're always bumping up against that. Our own pain is always more important to us than the pain of others, and it's far too easy to look away from the needs of others. We've all been hurt in one way or another by those who should have cared for us but didn't. And we've all probably hurt others because there were times when they were looking for compassion from us and it didn't come.

One of the problems in our society is "over-communication." We are deluged with images of so many hurting people and exposed to so many violent scenes that sometimes we become numb to it all. I don't watch much TV, except the news, but even the evening news bombards me with so many accidents, tragedies, and acts of violence that it becomes very easy for me to look away unmoved. That's not good.

As a Christian I feel this tension between compassion for those who need it and numbness because I've seen too much need.

If compassion is a mark of well-being, then I'm dealing with a lot of competition to that wellness. How about you?

Reflecting on God's Word

Jonah 3:10-4:3
Matthew 25:31-46
Galatians 5:22-6:10

For Further Reflection

1. Read Matthew's brief account of Jesus' compassion (9:35-38). Try to imagine what was happening in the heart of Jesus. How did he feel? What did he do?

2. Remember a time when someone expressed compassion toward you. Why do you think he or she treated you that way? How did you feel? Did it make a difference for you?

3. Intentionally look for someone who needs compassion today, perhaps someone you might otherwise easily overlook. Show your compassion to that person in a way that will encourage and help him or her.

5. Hope

My mother was a very quiet woman, usually quite reserved. You wouldn't find her in the center of a lot of activity or conversation. That's reasonable when you consider that she had debilitating pain for most of her adult life. When she passed away at age eighty-one, she had spent about half of her life severely limited with rheumatoid arthritis and in constant pain. She attended my college graduation in a wheelchair. Consequently she knew her share of depression, probably more than her share.

But at certain times in her life—when she was scheduled for reconstructive surgery—the flame of hope began to burn more brightly. Oh, she knew the surgeries would not be pleasant and would bring more pain for a while. But for my mother they opened the door of hope. A disease like rheumatoid arthritis goes only in one direction—downhill. The deterioration gets steadily worse. For her the surgeries brought hope of reversing the deterioration. First it was a knee, then another knee, one hip, the other hip, hands, neck—my mother endured thirteen such surgeries over the years. She never complained. Those surgeries gave her hope to get out of her chair again, to walk again, to go out again.

We all need hope.

Swiss theologian Emil Brunner once observed, "What oxygen is for the lungs, such is hope for the meaning of life." A noted cardiologist said, "Hope is the medicine I use more than any other." And in the words of King Solomon, "Hope deferred makes the heart sick, but a longing fulfilled is a tree of life" (Proverbs 13:12).

Hope says, "Tomorrow will be at least somewhat better than today." "My deepest fears will not materialize." "I will be able to manage what now seems unmanageable." "The road into the future does not go downhill steadily; it turns upward." "We can find a way that will be better."

Such hope gives steadiness to many who, like my mother, carry heavy burdens. It directs an immigrant family, like my father's, from one land to another in search of a better life. It allows people who have suffered more than the rest of us can imagine to endure and enables millions of believers to travel through the valley of death with great anticipation.

Hope comes when we realize that life is not ultimately in our hands. When we trust the God who rules over all. When we believe that God is benevolent and faithful. When we are sure that God walks with his arm around us, weeps with us in our pain, and promises to see us through. Hope is knowing the resurrection of Christ and hearing God call him the "firstfruits."

Hope is believing that "God is faithful; he will not let you be tempted beyond what you can bear. But when you are tempted, he will also provide a way out so that you can endure it" (1 Corinthians 10:13).

My mother trusted that promise. She went to be with the Lord in 1990. She fully understands it now.

The Christian faith is uniquely saturated with hope. In Christ we are freed from our sins and guilt, we are assured of loving care through the storms of life, and we can be confident that he is on the throne of the universe. We know that nothing will separate us from Christ's love and that glory awaits us at the end of life's road.

We are the healthiest when we have hope like that.

Reflecting on God's Word

Psalm 16
Romans 8:18-25
Hebrews 6:13-20

For Further Reflection

1. Write down as many Scripture texts as you can find in fifteen minutes that speak about hope. You might want to use a concordance or a study Bible.

2. Recall a time in your life when you lost your sense of hope. What caused you to lose it? What or who helped you to find it again?

3. Look around in your neighborhood, your family, or your church and identify one or two people who probably have difficulty feeling hopeful today. What could you do to encourage them this week?

6. Faith

Through the years, I've struggled a lot with the whole matter of faith. I imagine that you have too.

Oh, I don't mean what we call saving faith—putting ourselves in the hands of Jesus Christ for salvation. I don't have struggles about that. I am just as sure as can be that I belong to him. I mean the other part of faith—trusting God in all the confusing, mixed-up events of life. That's the part that often throws me for a loop.

Life just seems so unfair at times. I've had my share of personal pain. I've seen my parents go through agonizing turmoil. I've stood by friends whose lives were shattered by accidents. I've stood by other friends whose loved ones were torn away by disease and lost some friends that way myself. I've watched parishioners whose high hopes for their family were smashed to bits and pieces.

Lewis Smedes wrestled with that too. I have always admired his writings as very honest and insightful because he was willing to admit that believing didn't come easy for him either. He saw and experienced his share of pain. His own life was abruptly ended by an unfortunate household accident. I've never forgotten his statement that the best kind of believing is "believing against the grain." When everything in your system wants to shout no, yet you continue to trust God. That's real faith, Smedes said. I've never forgotten that.

So every once in a while I feel like I have to go for a boat ride with the disciples. The story is in Matthew 8, Mark 4, and Luke 8. The fact that it shows up in three places makes me think God is determined that I get the point! Here they are in the storm. The boat is getting swamped. Jesus is sleeping, and the disciples are afraid that they are about to drown. Ever feel that way?

The disciples go and wake Jesus up from a sound sleep. A terse verbal exchange follows. They say, "Master, we're going to drown!"

Jesus gets up and rebukes the wind and the waves. And then he says to the shaken disciples, "Where is your faith?" (Luke 8:24-25).

The disciples' words were an expression of their anxiety. Jesus' words were a rhetorical challenge. He knows they have faith, so this isn't an inquiry. It's really a challenge for them to take their faith and put it to work even in these scary circumstances. As Lewis Smedes said, you do your best believing when you do it in a storm.

If we could ask Jesus what he really meant by his question "Where is your faith?" I think he'd say something like this: "Go ahead and look at the storm . . . don't deny it. Then take your faith and put it to work so that you rise above your tendency to panic. Look at the storm, even at all the water coming into the boat, and then look at me! Look at me and remember that you belong to me!"

That's real faith. Looking at Jesus in the storm and remembering that we belong to him.

Reflecting on God's Word

Psalm 37:1-8
Romans 8:28-39
Philippians 4:10-13

For Further Reflection

1. Think of a recent storm you experienced. What might have caused you to panic? What helped you trust?

2. Reflect further on Lewis Smedes's comment that the best believing is believing "against the grain." What do you think he meant? What message is there for you today?

3. Think of someone near you who is in a storm right now. Pray for the strength of his or her faith right now. And then come up with some way to encourage this person.

7. Passion

I'm a habitual reader of signs and messages. License plates, bumper stickers, church signs—any kind of message board. They all catch my eye. A good bit of the time that's wasted effort; so many of them are inane. But every once in a while a real gem comes along.

On the way home from the dentist the other day, I passed a good one: "Even if you are on the right track, you'll get run over if you just sit there." I smiled. Then I chuckled. (You'd chuckle too if I told you this sign was in front of we used to call a "rest home.")

It's worth recalling this gem of wisdom in every chapter of life.

I really admire all the passionate people I've worked and ministered with. But I've also seen many people of all ages who seem so unmotivated. They desire no demanding goals—nothing that might call the highest and the best out of them. They sit in church pews Sunday after Sunday but you can't seem to ignite any kind of spark in them. A lot of seniors are that way too. They allow themselves to think that this chapter in life is for taking it easy. They're the ones who say, "I've done my part; now it's time for others." They sign off to merely watch . . . and risk getting run over.

People without passion are not healthy. And they are a drag on the church.

Passion is a word that gets a lot of bad press. Many people bear the scars of too much erotic and angry passion. But I'm convinced God created us with the capacity for healthy passions. If we fail to live by them we deny the image of God in us and we lose our health and wellness.

If you want to meet a fellow with passion, spend some time reading the apostle Paul. He had a passion to travel the world with the truth, to preach the gospel, to reach the lost, to plant churches, to become all things to all people. You'd never find Paul just sitting on the track!

Paul was also passionate about passing on that fervor to others. "Whatever you do," he advised, "work at it with all your heart, as working for the Lord" (Colossians 3:23).

Paul was writing this advice to slaves about the kind of Christian slaves they ought to be. He was also talking to masters about the way to be a Christlike master. But the context suggests he also had fathers and mothers and boys and girls in view. As a matter of fact, he ties it all to the resurrection of Christ and to our participation in his resurrection. Since Christ is raised, and we are risen with Christ, life is different—right here, right now. We are not only on a different track but we refuse to sit down on the track.

Risen people are passionate people.

Passionate people tend to be healthy people.

And passionate people help create healthy communities and churches.

Reflecting on God's Word

Hosea 11:1-11
Romans 12:1-13
1 Corinthians 13

For Further Reflection

1. Select a person whose healthy Christian passion has been a model for you. What is that passion and how do you see it expressed? Stop right now and thank God for this person.

2. What are your deepest Christian passions? What draws the best out of you, and for what causes are you willing to give yourself fully? Are you responding to that passion the way you ought to?

3. In Colossians 3:1 Paul ties all this to our identification with Christ in his resurrection. Try to explain how being "raised with Christ" does and should shape your passionate involvement in God's kingdom.

8. Partnerships

I've long been intrigued by the story recorded in Mark 2. It's the story about a man who was paralyzed and was healed by Jesus when some men lowered him through the roof. Just imagine how much fun it would have been to be one of the people crowded into the room with Jesus—riveted on the words of Jesus, we're abruptly interrupted by debris falling on our heads. We look up, and, lo and behold, there's a fellow on a cot coming down right in our midst!

But this is a story in which the secondary details carry a big message. Usually in this story people focus on Jesus the healer or the paralyzed man who experienced healing or perhaps even the perpetually argumentative teachers of the law.

But I'm drawn to four unnamed people in the shadows. We have no information on who they are. All we know is what Mark tells us: "Some men came, bringing to him a paralyzed man, carried by four of them" (Mark 2:3).

These four actually play a central role in the story. They were unselfish fellows who were more interested in carrying their friend than in doing all the other things they probably had to do. They were also very creative—most people probably wouldn't have thought to solve the crowded-house problem by coming down through the roof. And they were cooperative partners. I can picture myself on that cot, a rope on each corner, a fellow on each rope—and one of them isn't paying careful attention. It could have made one very unceremonious drop in front of Jesus!

A careful reading of the story shows that Jesus considered these four men heroes—heroes of faith. They would have fit right in with the list of heroes in Hebrews 11. Verse 5 says that the man who was paralyzed was healed "when Jesus saw their faith." *Their* faith—plural! The faith of the man's friends made a key contribution to the healing he experienced.

That always gets me thinking. It makes me realize how important other people are to each of us. How the faith of others may well have made a greater difference in my life than I realize. How my life and ministry would have been much poorer were it not for certain people who "carried my cot." I picture those people who have pulled up alongside me to encourage me, work with me, and sometimes even carry me. I think about my family, my friends, and my colleagues on staff in the pastorate. And I wonder how many of God's blessings I experienced because of *their* faith.

But then I turn it around, and I wonder how much I've been a partner to others. Have I pulled up alongside others enough to bless them? Has my faith opened the door for others to receive Christ's gifts?

Isolated people are poorer than those who are surrounded with partners in Christian service. And those of us who are partners with many others must be the healthiest people around.

Reflecting on God's Word

Ecclesiastes 4:7-12
1 Corinthians 12:12-25
Philippians 1:3-11

For Further Reflection

1. Remember five people who have been your best "faith partners" in living the Christian life. Give thanks to God for them. Then send them each a message, either by email or snail mail, to express your appreciation for them.

2. Think of five people for whom you have tried to be a faith partner. Pray daily that your encouragement to them may bring more of God's goodness into their life.

3. Observe people around you. Who is alone, like the man who was paralyzed lying on his cot and very much in need of some faith partners? How can you and some of your friends step into that role?

9. Forgiveness

Few things sap the health and happiness of Christians more quickly than grudges and resentments. Nothing drains us of our spiritual strength more than our refusal to practice the Christian art of forgiveness.

I have been surprised at how often relationships in our churches are marked by fractures, harbored offenses, and nursed grudges. Surprised too at how easy it is for me to fall into this trap.

How strange! At the very heart of the Christian gospel we treasure is the act of God's gracious forgiveness. Christianity is all about forgiveness. Wouldn't you expect Christ's body, the church, to be a shining light of forgiveness practiced in our society?

It's clear that Jesus expected that when he taught his followers to pray "forgive us our debts, as we also have forgiven our debtors" (Matthew 6:12).

Or maybe he taught us to pray for forgiveness because he knew it would be such a problem. Maybe he understood just how hard it would be for us to forgive one another. Perhaps he knew that "I'm sorry" can be two of the hardest words to speak, and "I forgive you" can be equally hard. Perhaps that's also why the Spirit led Paul to write, "Be kind and compassionate to one another, forgiving each other, just as in Christ God forgave you" (Ephesians 4:32).

Either way, the practice of forgiveness, of extending to others what Christ has extended to us, is a vital Christian discipline no healthy Christian can live without.

Perhaps forgiveness must begin with self-forgiveness. So many Christians who have been freely forgiven by God seem to find it so difficult to forgive themselves. They go on chastening themselves for sins that Christ has forgiven long ago.

More obvious is the forgiveness we must extend to others who have hurt us. We all bear wounds and scars from harsh words and abusive treatment at the hands of others. No matter whether these people meant us harm or not, we remember the event and we hold it against them, making our relationship difficult, if not impossible.

Sometimes we justify our failure to forgive on the basis of the severity of the wound or the person's refusal to ask for forgiveness. But our lack of forgiveness harms us and our health more than it harms others.

Sometimes we need to let go of past hurts in the spirit of "bearing with one another in love" (Ephesians 4:2). We need to apply the oil of grace to smooth the rough edges of a relationship. Other times we need to respond warmly to an apology with intentional efforts to rebuild a relationship. We need to let go of the desire for revenge, even though a fully restored relationship may not be possible at this time. We need to extend the open hand of a willingness to forgive even if there is no response from those who have offended us.

For our own well-being, we must cleanse our hearts of the damaging spirit of grudges and resentments.

Reflecting on God's Word

Psalm 32
Matthew 6:14-15
Luke 15:11-32

For Further Reflection

1. What sins of your past are you still holding against yourself, even after you have confessed them to God? Write them down. Then burn the paper as a visual reminder that they are truly gone. Live in freedom from guilt.

2. Think of a time when you have offended someone. It's not too late to apologize and ask for the person's forgiveness in a personal conversation, phone call, email, or a note.

3. Recall a situation where someone who offended you and has never asked for forgiveness. Resolve today that you will release the resentment you are holding. Provide for your health by extending a forgiving heart toward this person and set aside any desire for revenge.

10. Prayer

James Montgomery's historic Christian hymn "Prayer Is the Soul's Sincere Desire" includes the lines "Prayer is the soul's sincere desire unuttered or expressed. . . . Prayer is the Christian's vital breath, the Christian's native air. . . ."

I often wish it were easier to pray—as easy as taking our vital breaths.

I'm not talking here about "saying prayers." That's not so hard. I've done that since I was a small child, and maybe you have too. We learned certain phrases, strung them together, and felt we had prayed. But is that really the kind of prayer suggested in the words of Montgomery's hymn? Is that what praying is all about?

At heart, praying is talking to God. Just talking. It's not really intended to be a formal liturgical exercise of getting just the right phrases in just the right tone. If that's the case, shouldn't we find prayer natural and easy?

Even Jesus' disciples, who spent so much time just talking with Jesus while they were walking along the paths of Galilee together still felt the need to ask, "Lord, teach us to pray" (Luke 11:1).

A little while later, Jesus apparently knew that the disciples were having a problem with their praying. He sensed they were tempted to give up, lose heart, drop out. Just quit. "Then Jesus told his disciples a parable to show them that they should always pray and not give up" (Luke 18:1).

He told them the story we call "The Parable of the Persistent Widow," about a widow who was incredibly persistent in beating on the door of a judge. The message is, "Hey guys, never lose heart!"

Talking usually includes all kinds of things: telling a story, asking for something, expressing feelings like love or anger and frustration, and simply listening. If talking to each other includes so many different kinds of expressions, surely our conversation with God involves all of those same kinds of expressions. Sometimes we might want to tell God about our day or ask him to help a friend or give him thanks for his gifts. Other times we might want to ask God for help in raising our children or call out on behalf of people around the world who are starving and suffering or tell him that life doesn't seem fair. You can add to the list.

We can pray this way because we really do believe God is interested in all those things. He gives us the right to tell him everything, even when we're struggling or angry. The audacity of prayer is believing that God really hears us.

But this kind of praying takes faith—lots of faith. After all, we're talking to an invisible person who never talks back the way we wish he would. Sometimes God doesn't seem to be responding at all. That's why it takes believing to pray and it takes faith to keep at it, even when something inside seems to be saying, "Ahh, just quit . . . God knows everything anyway!"

The greatest audacity of all, it seems to me, is believing that God really does want to hear from me, and he misses it when I lose heart or get "too busy" to pray.

Reflecting on God's Word

2 Chronicles 6:12-21
Psalm 5
Philippians 4:4-7

For Further Reflection

1. Is your prayer life is better or poorer today than it was five years ago? If better, what has helped it? If poorer, what has caused it to slip?

2. What is your greatest struggle with prayer: some struggle with God and his ways, or some theological question about its importance, or your schedule, or your motivation, or . . .? Try to clarify what could be standing in the way of greater prayer health.

3. How much of your praying is asking something *from* God, instead of giving thanks and praise *to* God? How much is focused on yourself instead of on other people and their needs? What changes might you need to make?

Formation

Most of us at some point begin to ask ourselves questions about what influences have shaped us into the people we are. Nearing midlife seems to bring on that question, but thoughtful persons ask it long before.

What has shaped the DNA of my personality, my view of life, my outlook on religion? Why do I consider this important and that frivolous? Why do I look for a certain kind of person as my friend, and why can't I tolerate certain other kinds of persons? Where did I learn to be suspicious of some people and to trust others?

More fundamentally, what shaped my view of who God is? What taught me to fear him or love him or wonder about him? How was my concept of Jesus or the Holy Spirit formed? What experiences have led me to believe this world is a safe place . . . or not? What formed my view of what life is all about and what I ought to try to accomplish?

Those are good questions to ask.

But even as we look at what has formed us into who we are, it's important to realize that we are still being formed. It doesn't matter if we are eighteen or fifty-three or seventy-nine. We are all still in the process of being formed.

You are not who you were fifteen years ago or even three years ago. I'm not either. Each year and each stage of life includes new influences that shape and reshape us, that cumulatively create the "us" in each new chapter in life. No matter where we are in life, near the beginning or near the end, we are still being formed and re-formed.

In this section I'll be reflecting on some of the most helpful formative practices I've found—practices that help us to live well.

If we are formed well, we'll be better able to handle the storms that life brings. On the other hand, the storms of life do their own work in forming our character so that we are able to live more richly!

1. Lifelong

Some tasks are ordinarily intended for only a certain time of life. We learn to walk, for instance, during the end of the first year of life. Elementary education is intended for our preteen years; high school for our teen years. In childhood we learn to ride a bike; in high school we learn to drive a car.

But the longer I live, the more I realize that other tasks cannot be limited to a certain period of life. I used to think that learning to talk and developing verbal skills was pretty well limited to childhood and adolescence—until I found that effective people continue to develop and hone their verbal skills. When I was in my early twenties, I assumed that I had most things in life figured out pretty well. At forty I began to realize that was not the case at all. At sixty, I knew for sure that wasn't true. Learning is lifelong.

Some pastors assume that learning, researching, and growing are for the first half of their ministry. From there they can rest on what they've accomplished already. Others believe that learning, researching, and growing are lifelong pursuits. They tend to be much more effective.

Parishioners have given me valuable insight into their experiences too. Many people assume that spiritual growth and formation happen only during the early chapters of life. But I recall conversations with two parishioners who shattered that myth.

The first conversation took place during a pastoral visit at a parishioner's home. I was much younger than he was. We were talking about his faith, his assurance, his joys, and his struggles. He surprised me by admitting that he has a greater struggle with temptations to sin and a greater tendency to doubt now, in his sixties, than he did in his twenties. He went on to explain that he'd always assumed that by the time you get past mid-life, things really settle down and go smoothly. Not so for him. It made me take a second look at some of my own assumptions.

The second conversation happened after a service at my church planned and led by the youth group. We encouraged them to express their own style and to focus on their own concerns and issues. After this particular service, a godly eighty-two-year-old member of the congregation, one whom I considered to be very mature in Christ, came to me with a very pointed observation. "Don't ever forget," she said, "that it's not just kids, but also those of us who are older often have a very tough time living the Christian life."

Both of those conversations reshaped my concerns. Why have we assumed that spiritual formation is an urgent concern only in the early decades of life? Why do we offer more Bible studies for youth than for adults? Why did I have permission to quit church education when I had made a public profession of faith? Why do we talk about discipling youth but rarely about discipling seniors?

And why does David find it necessary to pray, "Do not remember the sins of my youth" (Psalm 25:7) and Paul find it necessary to instruct Titus, "Teach the older men to be temperate, worthy of respect, self-controlled, and sound in faith, in love and in endurance" (Titus 2:2)?

Apparently being formed after the pattern of Christ is a lifelong process. I'm not finished yet. I look back at some of the experiences of my adult life and realize that those adult experiences have formed me as fully as anything in my adolescence.

I won't be finished until, at the end, Christ glorifies me!

Reflecting on God's Word

Psalm 90
Ecclesiastes 12:1-8
1 Timothy 1:12-17

For Further Reflection

1. Many people assume that most spiritual growth generally happens in the first three decades of life. What do you think about this assumption? Why?

2. What is Christ doing in your life now to form you more and more after the pattern of Christ?

3. Do you find it easier to live the Christian life now than it was ten or twenty years ago? In what ways is it easier? In what ways might you find it more difficult?

2. Amazement

Ahealthy dose of amazement can be the juice that keeps a life growing well. Amazement is to our spiritual formation what sap is to a tree. There is no healthy growth without it.

Our sense of amazement is fed and seasoned by our struggles with the ups and downs of our lives. When our eyes are open, there are so many things to be amazed about. How is it, for instance, that life courses through our body? That our lives actually reflect the image of God within us? That we are placed in just the right setting to be cared for? Ever wonder why good things sometimes come out of otherwise terrible situations?

And how is it that God cares for each one of us? After all, I'm only one of several billion people on this planet. Isn't it rather audacious to assume God is interested in me and what I'm becoming? Isn't it amazing to think that the creator of all things could take time for me?

That spirit of amazement is what attracts me to one of Jesus' most fascinating parables—the parable of the workers in the vineyard. You can read it in Matthew 20:1-16. All these fellows are hired to work in the vineyard—but while some work twelve hours, others work only nine, six, three, or even only one hour. As evening comes they all line up at the pay table. We expect their pay to be prorated according to the hours they've worked. That's the way business operates.

But not here. In Jesus' story, everyone is paid the same. Everyone gets a full day's wage—a denarius—the Roman coin for a day's work.

Some of the workers grumble. They think they should get more. Others are amazed. They got far more than they deserved and are thrilled at the generosity of the master.

The master brings them all up short with his reply: "Don't I have the right to do what I want with my own money? Or are you envious because I am generous?" (Matthew 20:15).

Surely most of us struggle with that. I, for one, am amazed. I'm amazed at the generosity of a master who would give a full day's wage to guys who worked only one hour.

I can just imagine this fellow running home, barging in the door with a huge smile, calling his wife, showing her the denarius with shouts of delight—"You'll never guess what happened!" I can imagine how he picked her up and twirled her around in a dance of celebration. And then did the same with his kids. Their home must have been riddled with amazement that day.

And I'm amazed at the God who treats me too with such overwhelming generosity—day after day, year after year!

That amazement is the lifeblood that constantly brings new formation to my spirit.

Reflecting on God's Word

Job 42:10-17
Psalm 33
Philippians 3:1-11

For Further Reflection

1. What is the most surprising gift God has given you in the past year? Where have you seen God's generosity the most?

2. Is it possible that you have lost your sense of amazement in life? If so, what has corroded it? How could you overcome that?

3. Imagine that you are the person who was hired at three in the afternoon. After fearing another day without work, you finally got called to work, and at the end of the day you received pay for a full day's work. Describe how you would feel. What would you say? How would you use what you were given?

3. Family

Most of the time we are unaware of the things that shape us. Even powerful shaping influences may not seem very striking at the time. But one influence that is certain to shape us is the family we grew up in.

Let me tell you about my family.

My extended family was a big one, especially on my father's side. I wish now that I could turn the clock back to some of our good times together. And I wish I had appreciated it more. My father was one of ten children (two others died in infancy) who immigrated to the United States in 1916. Times were hard. They had very little money or education. Sixth grade was as far as my father went in school because he had to go to work to help support the family. His brothers and sisters didn't get much more education. But they were powerful teachers. They taught us about living and believing and working and being true to what is true.

Church was a big part of our family life. We may have been members of different congregations, but when we gathered for the family ritual of Sunday morning coffee we'd flip our morning bulletins on the table for all to read. Vigorous discussions followed. The subjects were weighty: church, schools, politics, work, basketball, aunts and uncles, and faith. Laughter was common. We may have called it "coffee," but these were actually seminars about living well. There was no interest in prestige among us, only a hunger for integrity.

I wish I could go back there and relive some of those times. I see more and more that I am who I am because of what happened there.

The psalmist Asaph said, "He decreed statutes for Jacob and established the law in Israel, which he commanded our ancestors to teach their children, so the next generation would know them, even the children yet to be born, and they in turn would tell their children. Then they would put their trust in God . . ." (Psalm 78:5-7).

The psalmist must have had our family in mind when he said that . . . and yours. Here was a generation of ten immigrant children and two courageous parents working hard to carve out a new life. In doing so they got the idea across to the rest of us that who you are and what you believe is more important than how far you get ahead.

Today we are the second, third, and fourth generations of those folks. We've grown up, married, raised our children, entered our careers, and now we watch our grandchildren. It's a big crowd. We're much more educated now, and we're scattered around the globe. But we have an identity that has forever been shaped by the extended family circle that nested in Muskegon, Michigan, in 1916.

We don't usually speak in these terms, but what was given to us in this family circle is a practical expression of God's providence.

Reflecting on God's Word

Deuteronomy 6:1-9
Psalm 78:1-8
Ephesians 6:1-4

For Further Reflection

1. Think back on some times with your extended family? What do you recall about them? Identify three gifts they have given you, and thank God for them in your prayers today.

2. What disappointments have you experienced in your extended family? Are you able to forgive them? Try to think of ways you may have been formed positively through these disappointments.

3. What kind of legacy would you like to pass on to your children and grandchildren? What would you like for them to write about you after you are gone?

4. Transference

Some transfers can be incredibly difficult. I've found that the more tangible things are, the easier it is to transfer them. Last week I went to the bank and transferred $500 from one account to another. It took only a moment. Later, at a family birthday party, all of the guests transferred the gifts we'd brought to the birthday girl. It went smoothly and she loved it.

But when I attended school, the process of transference was more difficult. The teachers tried to transfer some of their knowledge of math and Latin into my mind. It wasn't always an easy process. Later on, my professor in college tried to get some deep philosophical concepts into my brain—with only moderate success.

When my children were small I transferred a few dollars into their pocket every Saturday morning—we called it "allowance." That always went well. But a little later, when I tried to transfer good driving habits to them, the process became much more complicated.

The most difficult transfer of all, though, is the one my wife and I took on when we presented our children for baptism. As a pastor I had the privilege of baptizing my three boys—a privilege second to none. As parents we publicly had to make a huge promise about transference. We had to answer the question "Do you promise to do all in your power to instruct these children in the Christian faith and to lead them by your example to be Christ's disciples?"

Now, as we watch our children attempting to do "all in their power" to do the same with our grandchildren, I realize how huge and uncertain a task that is.

The writer of Proverbs makes it sound so simple: "Start children off the way they should go, and even when they are old they will not turn from it" (Proverbs 22:6).

How do you transfer faith from one person to another? I know how to give a gift or transfer funds or even hand over my estate. But how do I transfer a life of faith? What's involved in such a transfer? My parents did it, and did it well. But what was the formula for their success?

I'm delighted that my three sons are walking with the Lord, but I'm not sure that I can take credit for doing certain things right. Throughout my ministry, I've often had to wonder why some very sincere Christian parents, who are so committed to this task, must live with the incredible pain of having one or more children walk away from the faith. It breaks parents' hearts.

No wonder we call it the "mystery of transference."

There are no easy formulas. Yes, it takes things like bedtime Bible stories and prayers, family devotions around the table, teaching kids to pray, and taking them to church. It takes letting our kids see us living out our own faith. It takes a big dose of Christian character, intentionality, teaching, loving, praying. Above all, it takes a massive dose of God's grace.

I wish I could explain how it happens. I can't. But when I see it happening, I am deeply moved to thank God. I hope you are too.

Reflecting on God's Word

Psalm 127
1 Thessalonians 1:1-10
2 Timothy 1:3-5

For Further Reflection

1. If you have embraced the faith of your family and parents, what attributes or characteristics made it most appealing to you? If your parents are still living, send them a note and express your thanks and love to them. Better yet express it to them in person.

2. If you are a parent, express to your children of any age—child, adolescent, or adult—either verbally or in writing, that there is nothing more in the whole world you would rather have for them than for them to embrace the Christian faith.

3. Think of other people besides your parents whom God has used to bring you to a faith commitment. Offer a prayer of thanks to God for each of them, and send them a note of thanks.

5. Meditation

I am amazed sometimes at how easy it is to lose our way in life. There are so many roads to travel, so many voices that call us, so many options to choose from, so many temptations that lure us. No wonder people lose their way—even good Christian people.

This lure to go astray may be especially dangerous during the first few decades of life when our values are being set and we are making basic life choices. But I haven't found any decade of life when this isn't a pressing concern.

I don't know how old Joshua was when he assumed the task of leading the Israelites into the promised land, but I do know he faced some big challenges. One of those was a constant danger of losing his way. So God gave him advice that all of us have needed ever since: "Be strong and very courageous. Be careful to obey all the law my servant Moses gave you; do not turn from it to the right or to the left, that you may be successful wherever you go. Keep this Book of the Law always on your lips; meditate on it day and night, so that you may be careful to do everything written in it. Then you will be prosperous and successful" (Joshua 1:7-8).

I am surprised at how often I've tried to convince myself that my daily time with the Word of God isn't all that necessary. After all, I tell myself, I already know the Bible pretty well, and besides, I'm really quite busy today. But God told Joshua that it isn't a matter of how busy you are or how well you know the Bible already. It's a matter of whether you want to stay on God's path throughout all the threatening distractions along the way. It's a matter of *doing* the Word.

Our hearts need to spend time in God's Word on a daily basis. "Meditate on it day and night," God said. So sometimes we choose to read a lengthy section of the Bible and other times we just chew on a special verse. Sometimes we read and then think for a while, other times we read and write down our reflections. Sometimes it happens at night, other times in the morning. Sometimes we feel the benefit of spending time in the Word immediately, other times it feeds our spirit in ways we're not consciously aware of.

Some people like to read the Bible straight through from Genesis to Revelation. I've never been able to enjoy that. It seems to me that God put a variety of literary genres in the Bible so that we can hear him speaking to us in a variety of ways. I like to read the Psalms once a year. Then I'll go to the epistles and the gospels. By that time I'm ready for some Old Testament history and maybe the prophets. Then back to the Psalms and epistles.

You may prefer another method—it really doesn't matter. Here's what *does* matter:

- We read because we know this is the voice of God speaking to us.
- We do so regularly and faithfully. There's nothing like a regular diet of God's Word.
- We listen and meditate on God's Word because we understand that these are more than words on a page—they are directives for staying on the right road.
- We read so that we can obey. "Meditate . . . and be careful to do . . ." God said to Joshua.

I can't imagine staying on the right path without listening daily to the voice of God coming through his Word.

Reflecting on God's Word

Psalm 1
Psalm 119:9-16
2 Timothy 3:10-17

For Further Reflection

1. How would you respond to someone who tells you that he or she is just too busy to read the Bible daily?

2. What is your favorite passage of the Bible? Explain why it means so much to you.

3. In past generations, most Christian families had the practice of eating meals together and spending some time at the table reading a passage of Scripture and praying. What do you think of that practice? Have we lost something valuable?

6. Gymnasium

I've never been much of an athlete. Fifth-grade basketball taught me that wasn't an option for me. Golfing in the rough more than on the fairway eliminated that one too. So I've been content to let others be the athletes.

Nonetheless, I've always been fascinated with gymnasiums. Especially gyms where people pay for the privilege of becoming a member so they can work out.

I've seen people enter a gym looking fine, well-dressed, and healthy. After a while these same people are grimacing, sweaty, and breathing heavily. Nobody seems to be smiling—they're all intense while they are working out. They actually seem to be in pain.

It makes me wonder why they would do that.

So I asked a few folks about that. I learned that while some people go to the gym just to have fun—maybe a game of pick-up ball—most go there because they see it as a means to a greater end.

The *end* is health and fitness. The means of achieving that end is training. They work out to achieve the greater health and fitness they desire. Some of them even hire a "trainer" to supervise their workouts.

I guess it all makes sense.

In life, some strenuous and painful means are necessary if we are to achieve the ends we desire.

As a parent, I've used some of those means to discipline my sons—not always the kind of discipline that involves levying punishment for errors and disobedience (though some of that too) but mostly just holding them accountable and helping them face the large tasks of "growing up"—tasks that require hard work and personal struggle. My parents did that for me too.

I've learned that God does the same thing with us. But it is one thing to learn it and quite another to accept and welcome God's discipline. In adult life I found it a bit more acceptable than I had earlier. Maybe by then I had been seasoned enough to see the necessity of it.

I take comfort in the words of Hebrews 12: "No discipline seems pleasant at the time, but painful. Later on, however, it produces a harvest of righteousness and peace for those who have been trained by it" (verse 11).

I find some solace in the words *later on*. There is something about the discipline we receive from God and from parents that requires the "later on" perspective. Discipline is always unpleasant and usually unwelcome at the time. But "later on" it begins to make sense.

I generally avoid gyms because I'm not one to work out. Give me a good long walk on a cool evening instead. But God has taken me to his gymnasium a good many times along my journey. At the time it wasn't very pleasant. I hurt and grimaced. I wished I could have avoided it.

But later on . . .

Reflecting on God's Word

Proverbs 3:11-12
2 Corinthians 12:1-10
James 1:1-8

For Further Reflection

1. Reflect quietly for some time and remember an occasion in your life when God allowed you to pass through a time of difficulty. What was the difficulty? Now try to identify what good came "later on" as the result of that experience.

2. If you have children at home, have a conversation with them about your practices of discipline and responsibility. Try to explain the growth you have in mind for them. Let them you know you understand it is painful at the time. Then ask them to explain their reactions and share their questions with you.

3. Why do you think some people become more angry and hardened through times of difficulty and discipline?

7. Self-Control

About three thousand years ago a very wise man said something we all need to hear repeatedly: "Like a city whose walls are broken through is a person who lacks self-control" (Proverbs 25:28).

That man was Solomon, and he might have avoided some of his own problems in life if he had done a better job of heeding that wisdom. Our lives, our families, our communities, and our churches would be better places if only we would pay more attention to Solomon's proverb.

Learning self-control is a key element of spiritual growth. It's a key ingredient in the successful process of formation and thus a key responsibility of parenting. Helping our children develop self-control is the single element that determines their success more than any other. I am more and more formed to be like Christ as I learn more self-control.

Some years ago an out-of-control freight train—horns blaring, reaching speeds of up to 110 miles per hour—came roaring down the mountain into San Bernardino, California. At a curve it jumped off the track, demolishing a neighborhood and snuffing out a number of lives. It was a terrible tragedy. The problem with that train was not with the horns or the stop signs or the laws governing trains or the barricades at crossings. No, the problem was *inside* the train—it was the brake system that failed. The problem was with the internal controls.

Solomon knew that internal controls for a person are like the protecting walls of a city. If the internal controls break down, the city is vulnerable to all sorts of enemies.

Imagine how different our homes, churches, and communities would be if our internal controls were always in place to put the brakes on powerful forces like lust, anger, greed, selfishness, and addictions of all kinds.

The apostle James speaks in terms of "taming" the evil forces within that are trying to get out. We put bits in mouths of horses to turn them. We use rudders to steer ships through the storm. But we have great difficulty, he says, in taming the human tongue. And because we fail to tame our tongue, much evil happens (see James 3:12).

Some people claim that humans are basically good creatures who, given the right circumstances, will always do what is right. I wish I could believe that.

The Bible teaches differently. The prophet Jeremiah knew that: "The heart is deceitful above all things and beyond cure. Who can understand it?" (Jeremiah 17:9). David knew it too. "Surely I was sinful at birth, sinful from the time my mother conceived me" (Psalm 51:5).

When my sons were first born I adored those boys too much to want to believe such dark things about them. And I'm sure my parents must have felt the same way about me—at least for a while! But we soon come to realize that the human heart is sinful, capable of more evil that we like to think. The only way to be formed into a Christian man or woman is to learn self-control—to practice good internal controls.

We hear about those with no self-control in the news every evening.

Reflecting on God's Word

Psalm 51
Galatians 5:16-26
1 Thessalonians 4:1-8

For Further Reflection

1. Call to mind some event in your life or your family's life in which relationships and witness were damaged because of the failure of internal controls. How could it have been avoided?

2. If we are all capable of evil because of our corrupt hearts, what should parents' priorities be as they raise their children to be healthy and productive persons?

3. What areas of life are you currently dealing with that require more self-control? Remind yourself of the damage that could result if you fail. Seek God's help and the help of others near you to be successful.

8. Going to Church

've gone to church all my life. Maybe you weren't raised in a family or community like that. Or maybe you've gone through a stage
of leaving the church for a while. Or you just consider it optional.

Not my family. We worshiped every Sunday. Skipping church was
just about as serious as skipping school—it happened very rarely,
and only for very good reason. Besides attending worship, I went to
Sunday school, attended midweek instruction classes in catechism,
and participated in youth group and all kinds of other activities. First
Church in Muskegon wasn't a particularly exciting church, but I cannot imagine my spiritual formation apart from it.

For centuries Christians have considered involvement in church
indispensable to spiritual formation. In church we learn to worship.
We hear the gospel of salvation and develop the ability to discern
between right and wrong. We gain a vision of what God is doing in
the world, sense awe in the presence of God, and identify ourselves
as part of the worldwide body of Christ. Without the church of my
childhood, I wouldn't be who I am.

So it's easy for me to understand David's cry from the heart: "One
thing I ask from the LORD, this only do I seek: that I may dwell in the
house of the LORD all the days of my life, to gaze on the beauty of the
LORD and to seek him in his temple" (Psalm 27:4).

I fully understand how and why the early Christians who were
converted at Pentecost "devoted themselves to the apostles' teaching and to fellowship, to the breaking of bread and to prayer" (Acts
2:42).

And it makes sense to me that the writer of Hebrews uses these
words to encourage the Christians: "Let us consider how we may
spur one another on toward love and good deeds, not giving up
meeting together, as some are in the habit of doing, but encouraging one another—and all the more as you see the Day approaching"
(Hebrews 10:24-25).

There were times when I resisted all that church-going. There
were times when I found it boring, times when I wished my parents

weren't quite so traditional. But now that a good many years have passed, I'm in a position to see that going to church had a richly positive part in my personal formation. And I'm deeply grateful that my parents insisted on taking me there.

I know that some people have been hurt or abused by the church. If you are one of them, I'm truly sorry. And I'm sorry if your experience of church has caused you to react against it, or if you were offended by the behavior of other members.

But let me say it again. I'm convinced that it's God's plan—and is the experience of millions of people—that going to church is a big part of being formed spiritually. If you've grown up as a churchgoer, you probably know what I'm talking about. If you are not a churchgoer, I hope you'll look for a church home soon.

Reflecting on God's Word

Matthew 16:13-20
1 Timothy 3:14-16
Revelation 7:9-12

For Further Reflection

1. Have an open conversation with your family or a friend this week in which you talk about why you go to church, what you hope to gain from it, and how you hope to honor God by it.

2. Some people expect the church and its people to be nearly perfect, and they are upset and offended when it becomes clear they are not. How do you handle that?

3. When Christians come to worship they engage in a "confession of sin" and receive God's pardon. What is the significance of that? Do you think it is necessary? Is it healthy?

9. Identity

German philosopher Arthur Schopenhauer was sitting on a park bench one day deep in thought. Along came a policeman who tapped him on the knee with his nightstick and asked, "Come, come now, who are you, and what are you doing here?" To which the philosopher answered, "Would to God that I knew!"

Many of us wish we knew! Especially in some seasons of life, the search for our identity can be pretty intense. I certainly struggled with it—long after others probably assumed I had it all figured out. And I've met many others who seem to struggle with the question of identity for years—some of them never quite arriving at the certainty they desire.

The process of spiritual formation includes arriving at a clear sense of our identity.

Who are we, and what are we doing here?

Through the years, I have come to realize that my sense of identity comes from many layers of influences:

My birth—The fact that I have been born into this family, this ethnic group, this century, this country says much about who I am.

My baptism—My placement in God's covenant family and the public declaration through the waters of baptism that I am a child of God gives me an identity that richly directs me. God's claim is on me.

My credo—I believe certain truths are eternal and nonnegotiable. I readily stand with others and profess my beliefs. I am formed by those beliefs.

My gifts—The Bible tells us that we receive the gifts of God's Spirit according to the purposes God has in mind for us and the way God intends to use us. I have come to know myself as I've come to recognize the gifts God has given me.

My calling—I haven't merely searched for a career that I'd like to pursue. Instead I've prayerfully sought out God's will and calling for me. My identity cannot be separated from my calling as a renewed child of God serving God and others in this way.

My personality—I don't know all the factors that influence our personality. I do know that I'm very different from some people I know and very similar to some others. The same is surely true for you. Having said that, we simply need to acknowledge that we are a unique combination of characteristics that makes us who we are.

My life experiences—Some of the people and events in my life that I've already referred to, including family, pastorates, and disease, have surely shaped my identity. You know the ones that have formed you.

I am sure that the list could be much longer—you can probably add some others. But no matter what factors we include on our list, I believe it is important that we see the hand of God working through all these layers of influences to form our identity.

The bottom line of our identity—all that really counts—is this: "If we live, we live to the Lord; and if we die, we die to the Lord. So, whether we live or die, we belong to the Lord" (Romans 14:8).

Reflecting on God's Word

Genesis 1:26-31
Psalm 139:13-18
2 Corinthians 5:16-21

For Further Reflection

1. Spend some time reflecting on the list of influences above. How has each of these shaped your identity? Which others would you add to the list?

2. Write, either in your journal or on the computer, a description of who you are. Use at least a few paragraphs (maybe more) to describe how you see yourself and what you consider to be your identity.

3. What negative experiences have impacted your sense of personal identity? What have you done to overcome these?

10. Friends

All of us need personal relationships. Those who have outgoing personalities may easily find friends and keep them; others, more introverted, may find these relationships harder to make and keep. Either way, our personal formation is significantly influenced by the kind of relationships we have.

Relationships, of course, don't just happen. We need other people around us, but that's just the beginning. We must be able to accept those around us and establish good ties with them. And we must be able to let them know us and look inside us. Forming healthy relationships is a two-way street—reaching to others with caring and love, and letting others know who we are.

Some relationships are established for us. We are born into a family, and our relationships with parents, siblings, uncles, aunts, grandparents, and cousins have a significant influence in shaping us for better or for worse. Other relationships—with people at school, at work, in the community, and in recreational activities—are accessible should we decide to pursue them.

Here we must be wise. For the sake of our spiritual formation, we must carefully filter those we allow into the inner circle of our lives.

My family had a powerful positive influence in shaping me spiritually. But during my adolescence I developed some friendships with the people I worked with that contradicted the values and patterns my family had set for me. Their life-view was the opposite of my family, and I was torn between the two. It was only when I moved away from those friends and deepened my relationships with classmates and roommates at college that my formation got back on track.

Too often in my ministry I've seen people who have developed close relationships with those who have formed them negatively. Hanging out with "the wrong crowd" has led some people to abandon their faith or leave the church. Still others have left their marriages or neglected their families because of the power unhealthy relationships had on them.

King Solomon, known for his wisdom, used a number of proverbs to communicate to his son the vital importance of having the right kind of friends:

> "A friend loves at all times, and a brother is born for a time of adversity" (Proverbs 17:17).

> "One who has unreliable friends soon comes to ruin, but there is a friend who sticks closer than a brother" (Proverbs 18:24).

> "Wounds from a friend can be trusted, but an enemy multiplies kisses" (Proverbs 27:6).

Our family, with all its weaknesses and failures, shapes us powerfully. But the friends and associates with whom we choose to have close personal relationships shape us just as powerfully.

One is given by God. The other we must carefully select.

Reflecting on God's Word

Proverbs 4:1-17
Mark 2:1-12
Romans 16:1-16

For Further Reflection

1. Recall three people—associates, classmates, teachers, coaches, youth workers, or others—who have had a positive influence on your formation. Give thanks for them. Consider sending them a note of thanks for their encouragement.

2. Now recall several relationships that you came to realize were unhealthy for your formation. How did you come to see that this relationship was not good for you? How did the relationship change?

3. Who do you see near you today who might be in need of a positive relationship to help form them spiritually? Pray that God will give you the correct opening to establish a helpful friendship.

Worship

'␣ve been a preacher all my adult life, so it's not surprising that worship has always been a big part of my life. But it started long before that. Church was a big part of my family's life: we attended twice every Sunday. My parents were deeply convinced that God wanted us there. They were convinced that none of us would be healthy Christians without faithful worship.

That kind of faithfulness had a lot to do with helping me sense my call to the Christian ministry.

Christians today are not necessarily convinced of that. Sunday often finds them in other places doing other things. Pastors notice a lower percentage of church members attending regularly than a generation ago. They feel like they have to work harder to keep them coming.

In this section, we will talk about worship as part of a healthy Christian life.

Worship means different things to different people—and rightly so. One helpful way to represent worship is by three concentric circles.

- In the very center is what we might call private or personal worship. That's the time we spend alone with God in prayer and in reading and reflecting on God's Word. Many people call this "quiet time."
- The second circle is corporate worship. It's what happens on Sunday when we gather in church with others who profess the name of Christ for a worship service. We gather for worship as the "body of Christ." (Some prefer to call "worship" only that part of the service in which we're singing our adoration to God.)

- The third and largest circle is the worship we give to God by living out our faith obediently all week long.

We'll use this image of concentric circles to guide our reflections on worship.

The more I live, the more my worship is saturated with a sense of privilege. Just imagine—God actually wants us to meet him in worship!

1. The Real World

He met me at the door at the close of the worship service. Shaking my hand, he said, "Nice sermon, pastor." I appreciated that. And then he added, "Now it's back to the real world!"

Real world! Did he really say that?

The man's comment got me thinking. Which is the "real world"? Is it the one out there where people raise their families, punch in every morning, try to keep their businesses profitable, deal with traffic jams, balance checkbooks, and handle life's daily stresses? Is it the one where our homes and families are located?

But what about the world "in here"? How about this world where we gather on Sundays in church to meet God, to sing and pray and confess and receive grace? Is this not the "real world"? About 43 percent of Americans, we're told, attend church or synagogue each week. Are they stepping outside the real world to do so?

How do we determine which world is real and which is unreal?

And which world influences the other? In the world of worship we are in touch with heaven and eternal things. In the world of daily living we are in touch with practical and earthly things. Does the world of earthly things influence the world of heavenly things? Or is it the other way around? What's at stake here is nothing less than our basic life-view—and our view of worship.

I've come to realize that most people think the real world is the practical and earthly one—and, implicitly, that worship is a rather unreal world. That perception easily shifts into thinking that worship could be labeled "irrelevant" or "optional." It helps explain why so many consider worship an "extra" to be engaged in only when convenient.

This is a major misconception.

The last book of the Bible helps us to straighten out our thinking on this matter. The book of Revelation is essentially about worship—the God we worship, the worship going on in heaven, and the hope worship gives us to cope with the suffering of this world.

The apostle John and his fellow Christians were enduring some tough times. Near the end of the first century the world had become a hostile place for Christians. The Roman emperor was angry that Christians would not engage in emperor worship. Their jobs and their lives were in danger. John had been exiled to the isle of Patmos for being a preacher. While there God gave him a book to write for the encouragement of all Christians throughout the ages. The visions of this book lift their hearts above the persecution and struggles of this world to see the "other"—the invisible world where it is clear that Christ is King, God is the Ruler, and victory is assured.

John begins with a beautiful vision of God on the throne saying, "Do not be afraid. I am the First and the Last. I am the Living One; I was dead, and now look, I am alive for ever and ever! And I hold the keys of death and Hades" (Revelation 1:17-18).

If that's just a fanciful vision that has nothing to do with reality, then the world John describes in Revelation is a false world. But if that is an accurate picture of a Sovereign God on the throne of this world, then what he is seeing is the real world.

The next time you come to worship God, remind yourself that you are in touch with that real world!

Reflecting on God's Word

Psalm 96
Ephesians 3:14-21
Revelation 4 and 5

For Further Reflection

1. Think about the reasons why you go to go to church. How could you explain this to your children or your friends?

2. As you enter the place of worship, think about how you picture God. What kind of a being does God seem like to you? Does that make you more or less eager to worship?

3. What do you expect to happen while you worship in church? In other words, by the time you leave, what will have occurred?

2. God on the Throne

Revelation is a rich yet mysterious book. We look to it for information about future events; we try to discern the course of events in our world. We hunger for some hope about the outcome of world history. We read Revelation eager to be reassured of Christ's rule, and we treasure the glimpses of the new heaven and the new earth.

The book of Revelation begins with worship—actually the first five chapters are essentially about the church at worship. It begins with pictures of the One on the throne and continues with pictures of those who are worshiping (with all their weaknesses). It begins *there,* not *here*—teaching us that heaven is the real world that influences this one, not the other way around. While we do our worshiping here in a hostile environment that is not particularly friendly to our faith, the book of Revelation shows us the throne room of God where worship continues unhindered.

In the first chapter of Revelation, we look around and see the object of our worship. We see the lampstands (the churches) and the stars (the messengers of the churches), and in the center the One who describes himself this way: "I am the First and the Last. I am the Living One; I was dead, and now look, I am alive for ever and ever! And I hold the keys of death and Hades" (Revelation 1:17-18).

John offers a symbolic description of a "son of man" who exceeds anything our minds can grasp in his holiness, majesty, and beauty. He was "dressed in a robe reaching down to his feet and with a golden sash around his chest. The hair on his head was white like wool, as white as snow, and his eyes were like blazing fire. His feet were like bronze glowing in a furnace, and his voice was like the sound of rushing waters. In his right hand he held seven stars, and coming out of his mouth was a sharp, double-edged sword. His face was like the sun shining in all its brilliance" (Revelation 1:13-16).

This holy being is the center of all worship in heaven! As we see shortly, all the angels and saints join in glorifying this Holy One.

A terrible tragedy has occurred in our time, as it often has in history. We have forgotten who is at the center of worship. We have too often thought that we are at the center of worship. So we preoccupy ourselves with matters about worship that mean so much to *us*. And we ask what *we* are getting out of it.

The pictures in Revelation tell us it's the other way around. We are not the center. The center is none other than the sovereign and glorified Jesus Christ, the Lord of the universe. We so often make the mistake of thinking of worship as a human event—as though we are attending a concert or a program, or we are searching for God. Instead, worship is a holy encounter, a conversation with the triune God.

We'll learn more from these words in Revelation, but for now we must remind ourselves about who is at the center of all our worship.

Reflecting on God's Word

Psalm 96
Isaiah 6:1-8
Revelation 4:1-11

For Further Reflection

1. Is it OK for us to think about "how much we get out of it" with regard to worship? What could be correct in that? What is dangerous?

2. Try to come up with three personal practices for Sunday morning that will help you better focus on Jesus Christ, the center of our worship.

3. Faithfully pray for those who will be leading in worship this week so they will be able to draw the attention of all worshipers to Jesus Christ on the throne.

3. Joining the Hosts

I find myself looking around at others while I worship. And when I'm in the pulpit I take careful notice of all who are there. Perhaps you do too. After all, Sunday worship is a corporate event. We do not worship alone. We gather as the body of Christ—a group of people who are connected with one another. We sing and pray and stand shoulder to shoulder with others as we worship.

But usually we have a far too limited idea of the others worshiping with us. Revelation 4 and 5 reminds us to look around in a much more comprehensive way. Those chapters portray four groups that are joining me in worship. First is the Trinity: the Father on the throne, the Son shown as the Lamb in Revelation 5, and the Holy Spirit who facilitates it all. All three are there.

Second, a crowd of angels is present. They are represented by the four living creatures in Revelation 4:6-8 and again in 5:8. John tells us the crowd of angels is so large they are virtually innumerable (see 5:11).

Third, the church of all ages is there. In 4:4 the twenty-four elders represent the church of the Old and New Testament. They show up again in 5:8. In chapter 7 John describes how this crowd of the redeemed is so large that no one can count it.

All these people seated in church in front of me, alongside me, and behind me are part of the fourth group: young and old, male and female, new believers and long-time believers, some I know well and some I don't know, some firm in the faith and some seeking. Those of us living today are just one historic slice of the church of all ages.

Together we participate in this act that we call worship.

And there is something else I notice from the book of Revelation. We don't all do our own thing in whatever way we'd like. John points out that the church—both the redeemed in heaven and those of us on earth—follow the lead of the angels. They lead; we don't. "Whenever the living creatures [that is, the angels] give glory, honor and thanks to him who sits on the throne and who lives for ever and ever, the twenty-four elders [that is, the church] fall down before him who sits on the throne and worship him who lives for ever and ever" (Revelation 4:9-10).

Those verses help me think much more deeply about my worship life. They tell me that the heart and core of worship is about giving glory, honor, and thanks to God on the throne. That's very different from being concerned about me and my needs first. And they tell me that the direction of worship is established by the angels. They act, and whenever they do, the church follows.

The next time I go to church to worship, I'm going to think of the crowd that is involved. I'll remind myself of God on the throne as the center of all. I'll remind myself of the glory and honor God deserves. And I'll think of myself and other worshipers following the lead of the angels in giving him praise.

Reflecting on God's Word

Exodus 20:1-7
Psalm 95
John 4:1-26

For Further Reflection

1. Imagine what it might look like to see God sitting on his throne. How do you picture the Father? What might the Son, the Lamb who was slain, be like? How do you picture the Holy Spirit?

2. The next time you are in church, arrive early enough to look around you at other worshipers as they arrive and remind yourself that they belong to God too. Then close your eyes and imagine the hosts of angels who are also with you, and the whole church in heaven.

3. What do you think would happen to our active participation in worship if we really followed the lead of the angels as in Revelation 4:9-10?

4. Grace

Worship is all about grace. Take grace away and worship stops.

Perhaps when we are on our way to church we should remind ourselves that we are on our way to the fountain of grace.

If grace points to the overwhelming generosity that makes it possible for God to love sinners, to forgive those who don't deserve to be forgiven, to accept those who are not acceptable, then we are able to come to worship only because of grace.

There ought to be a huge sign over the door: ENTER BY GRACE ONLY.

We profess Paul's words "by the grace of God I am what I am" (1 Corinthians 15:10). If only we were more aware of that, it just might revolutionize how we feel about worship and how we participate. No longer would we be tempted to come only out of duty and obligation. No longer would we feel the pressure of needing to worship "just right" in order to win God's favor. No longer would we feel the heaviness that often seems to mark worshipers. No longer would boredom show up.

No longer would we focus on anything other than Jesus Christ, our gracious Savior. All eyes would be on Jesus. All praise would be given to him. All hearts would be rejoicing. All eyes would glisten with tears of amazement.

Just imagine. We would begin our worship with heartfelt adoration and praise. We could confess our sinfulness without hesitation because we know the fountain of grace is already overflowing and has washed all our sins away. We would treasure the huge moment when the pastor speaks God's words of pardon. We would allow God's promises to wash away all those dark corners of fear that we've harbored for so long. We would pray and know we were being heard.

Just imagine. We would celebrate baptisms. We would rejoice with parents who bring their two-month old child dressed in a family heirloom baptism gown and see the waters of baptism drip down her forehead. We would hear the baptism in the name of the Father, the Son, and the Holy Spirit, and we'd get a lump in our throat to witness God placing his name on this little one. We'd celebrate when a young mother professes her faith and kneels to receive the same water of baptism, glowing with the peace of knowing God accepts her—no matter what her former life involved.

Just imagine. We would come to the Lord's table for the sacred and joyfully solemn moment when bread is broken and wine is poured. We would feel heaven itself opening up when the pastor says those precious words *for you*—"The gifts of God for the people of God." It's one of those deep moments that is so rich it brings tears of joy and relief.

Worship is all about grace. Keep your eye on that as you prepare to worship this week.

Reflecting on God's Word

Psalm 116
Isaiah 53
Ephesians 2:1-10

For Further Reflection

1. Think about why you go to worship. Do you go there to win the notice and approval of God or others? Or do you go because you love God for so graciously accepting you? Reflect on God's grace that enables you to worship.

2. What are the feelings you experience when the sacrament of baptism takes place? What do you say after the service to someone who has been baptized or to those who have presented their child for baptism?

3. Describe your reactions after a recent service of the Lord's Supper. Have you ever felt hesitant about coming to the sacrament? If you could choose, what song would you want to sing after the sacrament?

5. Vertical Habits

Where I work, at the Calvin Institute of Christian Worship, we frequently talk about "vertical habits." These are habits we need to learn and practice in our worship. Sometimes we encounter resistance to the word *habits* as though habits are a bad idea. True, we must never worship "merely out of habit." Yet God desires to form us after the character of Christ by building certain structures into our lives. When those structures are part of our regular actions and practices we call them habits.

Habits can be very good things—especially habits that are vertical and exercised in our worship of God.

The habits of worship are important because the words and language we use are a large part of our worship life, just as they are a large part of life generally. With words we communicate, we teach, we ask, we reconcile, and we love.

No relationship can survive without the regular use of words like *I love you, I'm sorry, I'm listening,* and *Thank you.* But we also needs words like *Help me, Why?* and *What can I do?* That's why parents spend so much effort in teaching children not only to talk and use words correctly, but to use the right words at the right time. Healthy people have healthy word habits.

God does the same thing. He is a God who communicates verbally. Some of God's words have come directly, some through prophets, some through other people, and some in the person of God's only Son. Many of God's words are written down in Scripture so we can hear God's voice through the generations.

At the Calvin Institute of Christian Worship, we say that carefully learned words are the building blocks of good worship.

With the psalmist we say, "I love the Lord, for he heard my voice" (Psalm 116:1).

We say, "Against you, you only, have I sinned" (Psalm 51:4).

We say, "I will praise you, Lord, with all my heart" (Psalm 9:1).

We even say, "How long, Lord? Will you forget me forever?" (Psalm 13:1).

We are taught to say, "Speak, for your servant is listening" (1 Samuel 3:10).

And we ask, "What shall we do?" (Acts 2:37).

For the sake of ourselves and others, we cry, "Stretch out your hand to heal" (Acts 4:30).

Words sincerely spoken or sung not only express our worship, they also form our character.

In our worship we hear the Word of God, and we expect our preachers to prepare well so they can express it accurately, clearly, and engagingly. We also speak words to God. It is vitally important for us to be as genuine, truthful, and engaged in our words as we expect God and God's servants to be.

Reflecting on God's Word

Psalm 15
2 Corinthians 1:14-22
1 Timothy 2:1-10

For Further Reflection

1. The next time you are worshiping in church, look over the order of the service. Identify the elements of the worship service where God is speaking. Then identify the elements of the worship service where you and other worshipers are speaking.

2. Recall three ways in which your parents taught you how to speak properly and truthfully to other people. Did they also teach you to speak to God in worship? How? If not, how did you learn?

3. Find someone this week to discuss when a habit is bad and when is it good. How can we tell the difference?

6. Preaching

We were involved in quite an intense group discussion—call it a debate—about whether preaching has any value other than filling time in church. As a preacher, I was defending the sermon as one of the God-designed methods to feed our spirits, teach us truth, and form our faith. But the debate wasn't going so well. Other voices made it very clear that they felt that most preaching was a waste of time. I felt pretty uncomfortable.

Then one guy delivered what he clearly believed would be the knock-out punch. He leaned forward in his chair, looked me straight in the eye, and said, "I've listened to sermons for years, and I can't recall a single one of them!"

Trying not to seem defensive, I did my best to explain to him that whether we see it that way or not, the preaching of God's Word builds believers up. But deep inside I had to admit that I've sat through my share of boring sermons, and I've preached my share of them too.

In my attempt to answer his charge, I quoted Paul's teaching that "faith comes from hearing the message, and the message is heard through the word about Christ" (Romans 10:17).

And I told him about Paul's farewell address to the Ephesian church. Paul knew he probably would not see the Ephesians again, and he knew they would probably have a hard time of it living out their faith in a pagan world. With deep concern, he said, "Now I commit you to God and to the word of his grace, which can build you up and give you an inheritance among all those who are sanctified" (Acts 20:32).

This was one of those conversations that went round and round long into the night after I got home. I just couldn't get it out of my mind. I had preached hundreds of sermons to that fellow. Was it all wasted effort?

Then I thought about my mother. And my childhood. I was a healthy boy and managed to grow up well, perhaps a bit shorter than the rest of my friends, but healthy nonetheless. It struck me that my mother had cooked good meals for me all through those years. Meals that fed and nourished me and helped my body grow stronger and taller, develop in function, and fight off diseases most of the time. So I began calculating. For eighteen years, until I left home for college, at three meals a day (not counting all the snacks in between), she had prepared over 19,000 meals for me.

I remember sitting down together as a family to eat. I remember learning to enjoy eating. But except for Sunday roast beef, green beans, and mashed potatoes, I don't recall any of those meals. Even so, those meals did their work. I was fed. I grew. I became an adult.

I'm not making a case for sitting through sermons disengaged, but I'm convinced that God forms us by his Word, week in and week out, more than any of us realize. So I intend to stay there, under the Word. On Sunday, and in my daily quiet time.

It forms me.

Reflecting on God's Word

Isaiah 55:8-13
Romans 10:8-17
2 Timothy 4:1-5

For Further Reflection

1. Think about the difficult task that preachers have, writing sermons that are interesting and engaging for old and young alike, for those who are motivated to listen and those who are not, week after week. Write a note to encourage your preacher this week and promise your prayers.

2. Begin a practice of memorizing Scripture on the basis of your pastor's sermons. It's a good way to hide God's Word in your heart. Select a passage that was important in the sermon and commit it to memory. Keep a record of those you memorize. Repeat them to yourself regularly.

3. Recall what you can from a recent sermon. Write a couple of sentences expressing what God may want you to do in response to this message. Try to listen with new ears this week.

7. Listening

Early in my ministry I never thought much about ears in church. Or about the role of listening. I assumed that worship was *doing*: talking, singing, praying, giving. But as I've accumulated more experiences of leading worship, I've come to appreciate more deeply the role of listening.

So let's do some thinking about the kind of ears that we bring to church—the kind we brought last Sunday and the kind we'll bring next Sunday. After all, how much we "take away" from church is determined to a large extent by our ears.

Early in his ministry, Jesus told a parable sadly misnamed "The Parable of the Sower." It's really a story about four kinds of soil and how they received the seed. Jesus didn't end the parable by saying, "Be careful how you sow." Instead he said, "Whoever has ears to hear, let them hear" (Mark 4:9).

It's a parable about ears—ears that receive the truth and ears that choke the truth.

The phrase Jesus uses in Mark 4:9 appears multiple times in the New Testament, enough to show us how urgently Jesus felt about the stewardship of our ears. Using our ears to hear must be a large part of our spiritual discipline. Jesus is concerned about those who have ears but don't listen carefully and therefore never understand. It reminds me of the times my mother used to say I had "selective hearing." I've said the same to my sons when they were young.

Paul warns Timothy about the fact that some of his hearers will have "itching ears" (2 Timothy 4:3). Itching ears are ears that hear very selectively, picking up only what they want to hear. They encourage their teachers to give them myths and falsehoods that are easier to handle. People with ears like that "hardly hear with their ears," says Paul in his closing remarks in Rome (Acts 28:27). And he sees that as an expression of the callousness of their hearts.

Educators today talk about "active listening." It's an important concept in a culture where people spend far too much time passively sitting in front of the TV. In active listening, we intentionally focus and consciously receive. When we practice the stewardship of our ears, we hold ourselves accountable not only for hearing but also for receiving, processing, and retaining what we hear, and then acting on the basis of it.

Sometimes when I'm in the pulpit, I wonder what proportion of the ears that day are engaged and functioning the way they should be. I know that much depends on how well the preacher and the musicians have prepared, but I wonder if we realize how influential ears are too.

Ears can block our ability to worship. Or they can enable healthy worship.

Reflecting on God's Word

2 Timothy 4:1-5
Mark 4:1-20
Isaiah 55:1-3

For Further Reflection

1. Write a short paragraph explaining what you think Jesus meant by the phrase "whoever has ears to hear, let them hear." How would you phrase that in your own words?

2. What do you think Paul meant by "itching ears"? Do you see evidence of itching ears in our society today? In your own life?

3. How can parents best teach their children to listen well in church? If someone takes accurate notes during a sermon, is that proof they have listened well? Is listening a function of the heart, the head, or both?

8. Remember Your Baptism

Sometimes when we step outside of our own tradition, we pick up some fresh insights from our brothers and sisters in Christ.

When I was a child, baptism was always a special event. I was baptized as an infant, and I always considered that a great privilege. And I was thrilled as I baptized our three sons. But through the years, I've sometimes had the nagging feeling that it's far too easy to forget those baptisms. It's as if we say "There, that's done" and put it on the shelf.

At a conference I attended some time ago it was different. Reminders of baptism were everywhere. As worship opened we were called into God's presence with a reminder of our baptism in Christ. When we confessed our sin, the pastor first poured water into the baptismal font to remind us that we are free to confess because of our baptism. When we approached the table to receive the Lord's Supper, we came down the center aisle, passing by a large baptismal font. We were encouraged to splash the waters of baptism to remind ourselves as we took the bread and the cup that our baptism was the path to the table.

That emphasis on baptism felt fresh to me.

If you were baptized as an older child or as an adult, then you likely remember it well. But if you were baptized as an infant you probably have no awareness of the ceremony except what others tell you, or perhaps what you've seen in pictures from baptism day.

Baptism is far more than a ceremony. In baptism, I received promises from Christ. I received the Holy Spirit to lead me to faith. I was marked as a member of God's covenant. I became a member of the church. In my baptism, I received my identity as one who has been set apart as a member of Christ. It is impossible to overestimate the influence of my baptism in forming and shaping me as a child of God.

Paul says, "We were therefore buried with him through baptism into death in order that, just as Christ was raised from the dead through the glory of the Father, we too may live a new life" (Romans 6:4).

I'm grateful for parents who helped me treasure my baptism. I can remember my father's bass voice saying to me multiple times (often when I was tempted to misbehave), "Howard, don't you ever forget that you are a baptized boy!"

We didn't just *get* baptized. We *are* baptized people. Our baptism forms who we are. It ought to form how we look at ourselves, how we believe, and what we live for.

I'm thankful for a new and growing interest in churches to regularly remind us of our baptisms. By doing so they help us remember the vows we are called to make for "baptized living."

I encourage you to do the same. Remember your baptism!

Reflecting on God's Word

Genesis 17:9-14
Romans 6:1-14
Colossians 3:1-17

For Further Reflection

1. If you were baptized as an adult, recall where you were baptized, what your reasons were for requesting baptism, who was present, and so on. If you were baptized as a baby, ask your parents (if they are still living) to explain the event to you and to describe what it meant to them. If your parents are not living, talk with your siblings about it.

2. If you have young children, set aside a family time, perhaps at the anniversary of each baptism, to remember their baptism. When and where was it? How did you feel about it? What do you want your children to understand about it? What does it mean for them?

3. The next time your congregation has a baptismal service, listen carefully to the questions that are asked and the vows made. Use it as an opportunity to reaffirm your own vows.

9. Come to the Table

I had an appointment with the late Robert Webber, a well-known author on issues of worship. He was late for our appointment. After I waited in the hallway outside his office for a few minutes, he came rushing in, apologizing for his tardiness. Without going into details, he explained that he had spent some time with a troubled student. Then he surprised me by saying, "You know what I told him? I told him, 'Flee to the Eucharist!'"

It was one of those formative statements that has continued to teach me through the years. "Flee to the Eucharist!" The troubles of the young man's heart would be cared for best at the table of the Lord.

How different, I thought, than the way we so often understand and present the Lord's Supper as a rather stern and somber event we participate in only after we have carefully scrutinized ourselves to make sure we are prepared and ready to come. Here, instead, was the sacrament with a wonderfully warm welcome where wounded and struggling people could find healing and peace, a table where people could find refuge.

It reminded me of Jesus' words "I am the living bread that came down from heaven. Whoever eats of this bread will live forever. This bread is my flesh, which I will give for the life of the world" (John 6:51).

Ever since that comment by Webber, I've wondered whether I have really valued and appreciated the Lord's Supper as much as Christ intended I should. I'd really like to come to the Lord's table more often. I need a time of healthy nurture for my spirit. I want the sacrament to be a time of rich joy while I drink deeply of Christ and all he has to offer. I want it to be a time that stirs my emotions deeply. My spirit needs plenty of time at the table.

Perhaps the words of the Belgic Confession can help us appreciate the sacrament in that way. At the sacrament, "Christ communicates himself to us with all his benefits" (Article 33). Speaking of the sacrament, the Confession uses words like *enjoy, nourish, strengthen, comfort, relieve*, and *renew*. Those words paint a picture of a rich, deep, and healing experience.

After all, we have two lives in us, the Confession says. One life is physical and temporal, which we've had from the day of our birth. We usually feed it well, three times a day, and we care for it in scores of other ways. Our other life is a spiritual and heavenly one, which is given to us at our second birth. That life needs feeding and nourishment just as much as our physical life. Much of that kind of nourishment comes from the Lord's table. When the Israelites celebrated the Passover throughout their generations, it fed their hearts and nourished their faith to remember how God had delivered their ancestors from Egypt.

Speaking of our need of such nourishment, John Calvin said, "Our faith is slight and feeble and unless it be propped on all sides and sustained by every means, it trembles, wavers, totters, and at last gives way."

And so we come to the table: a seventy-two-year-old woman with all her struggles, a young father trying to find balance in life, an eighty-year-old still vibrant and eager to be nourished, a teen whose faith is growing, and an eight-year-old boy who knows for sure that Jesus loves him.

I love and need a good meal. All of us do. Especially the meal at the Lord's table.

Reflecting on God's Word

Exodus 12:24-30
Matthew 26:26-30
1 Corinthians 11:17-34

For Further Reflection

1. Imagine sitting around the family table for the celebration of the Passover. Listen to your father explain to you what this ceremony means (see Exodus 12:26). What emotions do you think you and your family might be experiencing?

2. Read 1 Corinthians 11 carefully. What mistakes/errors is Paul concerned about in the practices of the Corinthian church? How can we be sure we don't make the same mistakes?

3. Are you eager for the next time you celebrate the Lord's Supper in your congregation? Why or why not?

10. The Blessing

Most often worship services close with words of blessing called the benediction. Over the years of my ministry I have lifted my hands over the congregation and pronounced these words several thousand times.

But over those years my understanding of those words of blessing has changed. My experiences and sickness over the years has helped me to better understand how fragile we are and how dependent on God's care. In my work as a pastor, I participated in the lives of others, and when they gathered on Sunday I knew their hurts, anxieties, and fears. In my mind's eye I saw them holding up little white flags with the word *Help* on them.

Gradually I came to see those closing words of blessing as perhaps the most strategic moments of the entire worship service. In some ways, church is a "safe" place to be: we are protected, quiet, together with folks of like mind. The strategic and difficult transition comes once we leave and are thrust back into the everyday world where we face pressures and stress, where responsibilities and decisions await us, where we are called to live out in a sometimes hostile environment the kind of kingdom living that we've talked about in church.

Astronauts will tell you that the most dangerous moments of a space flight happen during reentry into earth's atmosphere. That's when heat caused by friction builds up to critical levels. The Columbia tragedy in 2003 illustrated that all too clearly.

As a pastor, I came to realize that reentry happens at the end of a worship service.

And so it became very precious to me to deliver the sacred words of promise from God to my parishioners. Sometimes this took the form of Aaron's words: "The Lord bless you and keep you; the Lord make his face shine on you and be gracious to you; the Lord turn his face toward you and give you peace" (Numbers 6:24-26).

Other times I used Paul's words of blessing: "May the grace of the Lord Jesus Christ, and the love of God, and the fellowship of the Holy Spirit be with you all" (2 Corinthians 13:14).

These words are not a prayer offered by the pastor, nor are they a wish that the pastor makes. These are words of promise given by God to his people.

Just as Aaron spoke words of blessing to the traveling Israelites as they crossed the wilderness toward the promised land, just as Paul gave a benediction to the Corinthians who had the difficult task of learning how to live out their faith in a pagan Greek culture, so pastors today offer these words of blessing to Christians called to live as kingdom citizens in a way that brings honor to their Lord and Savior.

Living out our faith every day is a tough task. So if you sometimes feel like Jacob, who wrestled with God and then said, "I will not let you go unless you bless me" (Genesis 32:26), you are right on target.

Don't miss those words of blessing at the close of worship.

Reflecting on God's Word

Psalm 67
Luke 24:50-53
Revelation 22:18-21

For Further Reflection

1. Discuss with your spouse, your family, or a group of friends whether the closing words of worship are a wish, a prayer, a hope, or a promise. How can you decide which it is? What difference does it make? Why does the pastor often have hands raised while speaking these words?

2. If you are a parent, when you tuck your children in bed at night and pray with them, consider giving them a blessing with the words of Aaron or Paul. Help them understand the significance of these words of blessing.

3. If this means that God's blessing goes with you, then does it mean that you have that blessing when you go to work Tuesday, or shopping on Thursday, or attend school on Monday? What difference does that make?

Praying the Psalms

t's hard to talk to someone you can't see. Hard to listen to someone who is invisible.

In that case, talking and listening to God is bound to be tough.

Yet we're taught that communicating with God is a core value of healthy Christian living. How can that be? How can we manage to succeed in talking with God? Is it possible to meaningfully carry on a conversation with an invisible being?

The Bible tells lots of stories of people who hear God talking to them—people like Moses, Samuel, Elijah, David, Isaiah, Mary, and many others. The Bible also holds up as models people who talk to God with the firm awareness that God hears them—people like Abraham, Solomon, Nehemiah, and Jesus himself. So we know that talking with God is both important and possible.

One book of the Bible, more than any other, seems designed for just this purpose. It's the book of Psalms. Psalms is a fascinating collection of writings—sometimes with God's voice coming to us, other times with our voice going up to God.

Even more fascinating is the wide variety of experiences and emotions you'll find there. Praise, thanks, confession, testimony, wonder, requests, cries, anger—it's all there. The psalms are wide enough to include all the experiences of our daily living and everything we might want to talk about with God.

The psalms give us freedom, for they assure us there is no time in life when we cannot talk to God with the confidence of being heard. The psalms are our teachers. They model for us how we can learn this difficult and mysterious discipline of praying.

I'm going to focus on some of my favorite psalms, the ones I've learned to love the most, in the hope that you will learn and be better able to identify your own favorites.

Read the psalms. Read them regularly, carefully, and thoughtfully. Don't be in a hurry. Chew reflectively on these few, and then add more of your own.

1. Belonging

Without doubt, Psalm 23 is the favorite psalm of many Christians. It has brought strength and comfort to generations of Christians in a wide variety of circumstances. When I lie awake at night, I often recite these precious words to myself. Perhaps you do too.

David the psalmist knew the life of a shepherd intimately. He also knew sheep and their habits better than many. Yet here David is not writing as a shepherd but as a sheep. In Psalm 23, he is not a shepherd who cares for sheep but a sheep who is owned by a shepherd.

David is writing his autobiography in Psalm 23. It's his story—a story of belonging. And he's encouraging us to make it our story too.

He begins his story this way: "The Lord is my shepherd, I lack nothing" (Psalm 23:1).

The Heidelberg Catechism puts it this way: "I . . . belong—body and soul, in life and in death—to my faithful Savior Jesus Christ" (Q&A 1).

David knew by personal experience that a deep bond exists between shepherd and sheep. He understood that nothing is more important for a sheep than to belong to a faithful shepherd. Without that security a sheep would become hopelessly vulnerable.

He knew that sheep are not very self-sufficient. They are restless, edgy, filled with anxiety, and easily agitated. They generally are not able to defend themselves against predators. They can lie down and relax only when they feel safe, secure, and well cared for.

The remainder of this psalm speaks about the benefits that come to sheep because of this bond—green pastures, still waters, right paths, comfort through the darkest valley, a table before enemies, and an anointed head. All are expressions of the goodness and love that form the relationship in which an owned sheep lives. They are expressions of the shepherd's special care, and David knew each of them in his own life.

This bond of "belonging" that occurs between sheep and the good shepherd is the basis of all our efforts at praying. Good communication takes place between people who belong to each other. Where there is no such bond, communication is bound to be shallow at best, perhaps even nonexistent.

As God's sheep, it's good for us to regularly walk through all these expressions of care that come to us through Jesus Christ, the good shepherd, and identify times in our lives when we have experienced them. What "green pastures" have you experienced? What "quiet waters"? What "right paths"? What was your "darkest valley" when the good shepherd helped you? Recounting these experiences goes far toward reinforcing our communication with God.

What I love best in this psalm is the fact that it's so open-ended. It never stops. The last word is *forever.* The loving care David celebrates in this psalm goes on and on and on.

Reflecting on God's Word

Isaiah 40:1-11
John 10:1-18
Hebrews 13:20-21

For Further Reflection

1. Find a copy of the Heidelberg Catechism (www.crcna.org/pages/ heidelberg_main.cfm) and commit Q&A 1 to memory. Recite it to yourself when you are awake during the night.

2. Remember the words of Jesus who called himself the good shepherd, and try to identify how Jesus provides for us all the benefits David lists in this psalm.

3. Try your hand at paraphrasing this psalm in your own words. In other words, if this is David's autobiographical testimony, write it in such a way that it is your personal testimony.

2. Praise

The book of Psalms is like a powerful symphony that reaches its climax in an exuberant burst of joy in Psalm 150.

From the first psalm to the last, the journey has been moving in this direction. Some of the paths along that journey lead through dark valleys, some through times of oppression and affliction, some through threat of enemies and attackers. Some psalms are a cry to God for help or forgiveness or at least some attention. Some are vibrant expressions of trust while others are cries of pain or even angry complaints. Still others are powerful testimonies of thanks for help given.

But in the end it all comes to this: "Praise the Lord" (Psalm 150:1, 6).

That little phrase uniquely characterizes the psalms—it is both an exclamation and an invitation. The psalmists know it's the right thing to do. God deserves praise because of his very essence and nature. God deserves it because of his mighty works and actions for our benefit. God deserves it because of his personal care of us and because of his rule of the world.

Read this psalm, paying close attention to the prepositions. Prepositions are the little words that we easily skip right over. I find three of them in this Psalm—*in, for*, and *with*. Those words are important.

With the first preposition—*in*—the psalmist directs our attention to two places where the praise originates: the sanctuary and God's mighty heavens. The first is local, the other is more expansive. The sanctuary was that place on earth where God and God's people met together in worship. In the Old Testament it was the Tabernacle or Temple where the Holy of Holies and the Ark of the Covenant were located. God's "mighty heavens," on the other hand, have no boundaries. It refers to the whole created cosmos, including everything and everyone God has created. Let praise come from everywhere!

The second preposition—*for*—points to the reasons for our praise (see verse 2). The "acts of power" point to the mighty things God has done for people, from the creation of the world, the deliverance from bondage in Egypt, protection from enemies, salvation through

Jesus Christ, to the rule of the entire universe. God's "surpassing greatness" points us to the nature and essence of God. It may sound a bit self-serving if we praise God only for what he has done for us, but when we praise him for his greatness we are doing it simply because of who God is.

The third preposition—*with*—reminds us that we use every possible kind of instrument to express this praise (see verses 3-5). The diversity of instruments here is striking. Someone has observed that by the time this psalm ends, it's a very noisy place!

As I read these words again, I wonder if the psalmist is feeling some frustration. He deeply desires that even more praise be directed to God. I feel some of that in my own prayer life when I try to praise God. My words seem so feeble, so inadequate until they are combined with music that gives them more soul!

I wonder if this psalm suggests a little homesickness for heaven where angels and saints and all of the renewed creation will finally join together in the praise we owe God. Think of how that will transform our praying!

Reflecting on God's Word

Nehemiah 12:27-43
Colossians 3:12-17
Revelation 5:6-14

For Further Reflection

1. Reflect on some of the attributes that make God worthy of praise. Write down five or six of those attributes. Then praise God for who he is.

2. Identify five "acts of power" God has done in your life. Write them in your journal and share them with someone. Praise God for these actions.

3. Evaluate your role in the worship music of your congregation. How heartily do you sing? What is your motive for singing?

3. Remember

Psalms seem to go in several directions.

Some psalms go "up." They are words directed from a human being on earth to God in heaven (wherever heaven is right now). When David says, "I will praise you, Lord, with all my heart" (Palm 9:1), he is speaking *vertically*—to God. When he prays, "Have mercy on me, O God, according to your unfailing love" (Psalm 51:1) he is speaking "up" to God.

Other psalms are spoken *horizontally*, that is, to other people. They are words of testimony, teaching, or encouragement spoken to family and friends. David testifies, "The Lord is my shepherd, I lack nothing" (Psalm 23:1), and he is directing those words to others around him. In Psalm 46:1, "God is our refuge and strength, an ever present help in trouble," the psalmist's words move horizontally and are addressed to others.

In our prayers we speak "up" to God, so our words are vertical. And in our testimonies of gratitude we speak to encourage others around us, so the words are horizontal. That seems natural.

Psalm 103 has always intrigued me because it doesn't fit into this pattern. David begins Psalm 103 not by speaking to God or to others near him about God. He begins by speaking to himself. His words are neither vertical nor horizontal; they are internal. "Praise the Lord, my soul; all my inmost being praise his holy name" (verse 1).

In this case, the antecedent of "my soul" and "my inmost being" is David himself.

The Holy Spirit is apparently reminding all of us, through David's example, that there are times when we need to talk to ourselves first before we engage in meaningful prayer. We need times of quiet reflection, times when we pull off the busy highway of life to remind ourselves of what we know but have too easily forgotten in the busyness of life. Over the years I've learned that I need to do that more and more. I can't help but think that God intended to use my time of sickness to remind me of that.

It's even more intriguing to me that David begins this psalm by warning himself about a great danger. The danger is that we humans have a tendency to forget things. That doesn't matter so much when we forget little everyday things, but David is concerned that we also easily forget the big things. Look at the list he comes up with to recharge his own memory: the Lord forgives, heals, redeems, crowns me with love, and satisfies my desires (see verses 3-5). Then he goes on to focus on the very nature of God as one who is compassionate, gracious, understanding, and faithful (see verses 8-18). Those are mighty big things to forget!

I need some time today to reflect and remember. If I don't deliberately remind myself to do that, I probably won't take the time. Then I'll be the poorer for it, and God will be overlooked.

I often wonder if my praying isn't going so well because I haven't disciplined myself to be faithful in remembering.

Reflecting on God's Word

Deuteronomy 8:1-20
Psalm 62
Luke 17:11-19

For Further Reflection

1. Spend some time sitting quietly and reflecting on the nature of God and the gifts God has given you.

2. Write down a list of five of the best gifts God has given you in the past month. Now write down a list of five of the best gifts God has given you in the first twenty years of your life. When you've finished the lists, talk to God about them.

3. Look for some other psalms in which the writer talks to himself first as preparation for talking with God. How many can you find?

4. Surprise

A healthy prayer life requires a sense of amazement and surprise.

If we only open our eyes to see, every day is full of amazing and wonderful surprises. I'm amazed at how vast the universe is and how tiny a hummingbird is. I'm amazed at how a seed of corn grows into a full ear and how a newborn baby grows into an adult. I'm amazed at the intricacy of the human eye and at the miles of blood vessels that run through our body. The longer I live the more I notice and am amazed by these things.

I'm also surprised that God pays any attention to me.

David wrote about his passionate sense of surprise in Psalm 139. It's one of those "I'm amazed" psalms. David's sense of amazement builds steadily throughout this psalm until he exclaims, "Such knowledge is too wonderful for me, too lofty for me to attain" (verse 6) . . . "Your works are wonderful, I know that full well" (verse 14).

If you dwell with David in this psalm today, you'll find him surprised about several big things in his life.

God knows me. Some of us may be a little hesitant to let others know the real person inside us, but David is pleased and reassured that God knows him thoroughly. God knows when he sits and when he stands, what he thinks and where he goes, what he says and what he plans. David finds it wonderfully reassuring to know that almighty God takes such a vital personal interest in him. Read verses 1-6 again.

God keeps me. All of us have times when we feel insecure and unprotected. But David knows it's absolutely impossible to be away from the protecting care of God. No place I go can ever take me beyond the boundaries of God's loving care and protection. I am safe wherever I go and whatever I experience. Read verses 7-12.

God formed me. Surely David could not have known much about medical science and the development of a fetus. But he knew it was God's work. "You created my inmost being . . . you knit me together in my mother's womb . . . your eyes saw my unformed body . . . all my days were written in your book." It's enough to evoke a hearty exclamation from David: "How precious . . . !" Read verses 13-18 and think of your own beginning.

To this list David could have added, *God remade me.* What David did not know to any great extent was that God would come to us in Christ Jesus and redeem us to be a new creation, dead to sin and alive in Christ. The full knowledge about that act of God was given to future generations—to you and to me. We know about the cross and the Spirit and God's rich salvation. We know he continues to remake us.

So be amazed today! Let yourself be surprised! Don't allow these great truths that are so familiar to us ever become commonplace.

Then go ahead and talk with God—in a spirit of surprise and wonder.

Reflecting on God's Word

Numbers 6:22-27
Isaiah 40:25-31
2 Corinthians 5:16-21

For Further Reflection

1. Sit quietly for a few minutes to let all the distractions disappear, and then slowly repeat these four phrases a number of times: God knows me, God keeps me, God formed me, God remakes me. Talk to God about your needs today with that in mind.

2. Memorize Psalm 139:5. Visualize God's hand laid on you, conveying a blessing to you. Repeat verse 5 numerous times today.

3. Pray these words from David: "Search me, God, and know my heart; test me and know my anxious thoughts. See if there is any offensive way in me, and lead me in the way everlasting" (Psalm 139:23-24).

5. Confusion

I assumed that by this stage in life, I'd pretty well have the big questions about life squared away. Some I would have figured out myself, some would have been answered by others, and the rest, I was pretty sure, would seem inconsequential. I didn't think I'd have to bother God with my questions anymore.

I was wrong.

At times I seem to have more questions now than I did when younger. True, I ask them in a different spirit now. And I'm more content to live with unanswered questions. But they haven't really gone away. I still wonder why some people who try to serve God have such a hard life. I wonder why Christians have to suffer as much as unbelievers. I wonder why those who thumb their nose at God seem to get away with it—even prosper.

That's why I feel so very much at home with some of the psalms. They give me freedom to pray with some confusion in my heart. They give me the right to live with questions and confusion.

Take Psalm 73, for instance. It's a psalm of Asaph, the leader of one of David's choirs. Asaph is a very honest guy who writes very candid and earthy poems. He's not the kind of person who tries to cover over his struggles so that everyone will see him as a well put together guy. He confesses to feeling envious of the arrogant who prosper in their wickedness. The wicked don't seem to pay for their wickedness, he says; instead they amass wealth and live free of care.

And when Asaph looks at himself and his attempts to keep his heart pure and do what's right, he wants to cry that it all was in vain because it didn't protect him from suffering. "What's the use of serving God!" he blurts out. "When I tried to understand all of this, it troubled me deeply" (verse 16). He expresses his frustration and confusion to God.

What a disaster if the psalm had ended there! What pessimism if that were the last word! But the very next word is *till*. It's a little word, actually a contraction of a conjunction, and therefore the kind we easily overlook. But it's the huge pivot for this entire psalm.

All these questions were oppressively troubling, Asaph says, "till I entered the sanctuary of God" (verse 17).

The Hebrews knew that the sanctuary was the place where the worshiper meets God, the place where the Holy Place and the Ark of the Covenant were located. They knew it was the place where God came close.

It's not so much that the psalmist suddenly got well-explained answers, but that he gained a new sense of the greatness of God, whose ways are too big for our little minds. He trusted in the justice of God, who holds all the wicked ultimately accountable, and in God's care for him.

The bottom line is that we don't live with answers; we live with trust in God. And so we can keep on praying.

Reflecting on God's Word

Psalm 27
Matthew 6:25-34
Romans 8:28-39

For Further Reflection

1. Identify three of the biggest and most troubling questions that you would like to talk to God about. Have you felt free to raise them with God? If not, why not?

2. Select one of those troubling questions and write a personal letter to God about it, explaining your question, honestly expressing how troubling it is to you, and asking God for some answers.

3. In Psalm 27, David felt all his enemies were surrounding him, tempting him to fear. What do you think he meant when he said that he wanted to "gaze on the beauty of the Lord" (27:4)?

6. Tears

Some time ago a deranged young man went on a shooting rampage in a small town. It was terrifying. A young police officer raced to the scene, only to discover that his wife and infant daughter were two of the victims. Some days later he was interviewed about that day and said, "I have cried so much I have no tears left."

I found myself thinking, "You think there are no tears left . . . but the truth is, sometimes we never seem to run out of tears."

Most people shed tears. Some of us have shed many. I've shed tears because of circumstances in my own life and because of the pain I've felt in the lives of others.

Some people don't know what to do with tears. We can't stop them, but we are embarrassed about them. We wonder if it's OK to cry or whether tears are a sign of weakness. And so we often try to hide them.

But are you willing to shed tears in God's presence? Can you freely give God your tears? Do they become a part of your praying?

The psalmists are open about their tears. They give us permission to own and to shed the tears life brings. You'll find no embarrassment about tears in the psalms:

"My tears have been my food day and night" (Psalm 42:3).

"All day long I flood my bed with weeping and drench my couch with tears" (Psalm 6:6).

In Psalm 56, David expresses his confidence that his tears never escape the loving notice of God: "Record my misery; list my tears on your scroll—are they not in your record?" (verse 8).

In each of the three psalms above, the psalmist is reaching for God. He is giving himself permission to feel the deep pain that often comes in life. Sometimes our tears are an expression of frustration or anger. But many of our tears are an attempt to reach for help and understanding—from others around us, but more often from God.

The beautiful message of these psalms is that God's help does come. There is safety in the midst of our tears. The sovereign God of the universe looks down and notices our tears. And not only does God notice our tears, but God is moved to compassion by them. God cares. He puts his arm around weeping people and tenderly holds them.

Jesus, our great High Priest, fully understands our tears because he has been here on earth and shed his own tears. He empathizes with us in our weakness, and we can be sure that we will find mercy and grace to help us in our time of need (see Hebrews 4:15-16).

It's OK to shed tears. No need for embarrassment. They may be a part of our prayer life. And while we shed our tears, we can trust God for help and care.

Reflecting on God's Word

Psalm 42
John 11:17-37
Hebrews 4:14-16

For Further Reflection

1. Try to identify what your heart is trying to say when you shed tears. I'm hurting? I'm afraid? I feel lonely? All of these, or something else?

2. Think of a recent time when you shed tears and felt embarrassment, or wanted to shed tears and didn't dare. Also remember a time when you were free to shed tears with someone else, but you were hesitant to bring them to God. Why did you feel that way?

3. Remember an instance in which you shed your tears, perhaps many of them, and someone cared for you lovingly. Who was that person? Thank God for him or her.

7. Patience

I've had to learn along the way that faithful praying takes a great deal of patience. Patience both in the sense of persistence and in the sense of waiting for answers to come.

While it certainly is true that God answers prayer, it's also true that God often answers them very slowly.

Perhaps there are things you've been praying about for years, and still you see no action. At times in my life I've reached the point not only of discouragement but almost of quitting my prayers because some of them seemed unanswered for so long. (I have one prayer request of God that I've been praying for nearly thirty-five years, and am just now finally beginning to see God's answer to it.)

Many people in Scripture had to do a good bit of waiting too. They had to wait for God's own good time. Abram and Sarai waited well past their old age for the promised child to be born. Joseph waited a long time before he saw his brothers come to Egypt. Zechariah and Elizabeth waited years for their first child. Mary and Martha had to wait two days before Jesus showed up after they sent him a message about their brother Lazarus being ill. Lots of believers have done lots of waiting over the years. And we're still waiting for Christ to return.

Faithful praying often takes patient waiting because God acts in his own good time. No wonder, then, that some of the psalm prayers include patient waiting: "Be still before the Lord and wait patiently for him" (Psalm 37:7), says David.

Surely that advice arose from his own experiences. In Psalm 13, we hear David crying out to God: "How long, Lord? Will you forget me forever? How long will you hide your face from me? How long must I wrestle with my thoughts and day after day have sorrow in my heart? How long will my enemy triumph over me?" (Psalm 13:1-2).

It's haunting to hear *How long?* so many times in one prayer. But those words represent the prayer life of every praying Christian at one time or another. It's a common theme of Christian living. In fact, when I turn to the book of Revelation and look in on the saints in heaven, I find they are still waiting. "How long, Sovereign Lord, holy and true, until you judge the inhabitants of the earth and avenge our blood?" (Revelation 6:10).

These saints are given a white robe and told to "wait a little longer" (Revelation 6:11).

Waiting a little while longer, until God's good time arrives, is a necessary ingredient of faithful praying.

But it's not just a matter of waiting, of passing time until God gets around to it. Rather our waiting involves submitting ourselves to the belief that God, who is eternal, takes the big view of things. God is not in a hurry. "From everlasting to everlasting" (Psalm 90:2), God works out his purposes from generation to generation. We may think we have only until next Tuesday but God has much longer than that.

Maybe that explains why Christ hasn't returned yet.

Perhaps we are touching here on one of the most sensitive aspects of following Christ in our praying. We need to surrender ourselves to a God whose actions are not as tightly scheduled as ours.

Faithful praying takes faithful waiting.

Reflecting on God's Word

Psalm 130
Luke 18:1-8
James 5:7-11

For Further Reflection

1. Remind yourself of other believers (in the Bible and in your own acquaintance) who have faithfully prayed for something while continuing to wait for a long time. What can they teach us?

2. List three requests you have made of God over a long period of time, yet seem to have received no answer. How are you waiting?

3. Recall an example of someone who has prayed for a long time about something, was tempted to give up (and maybe did at times), and finally did receive God's answer.

8. Honesty

Good communication is built on honesty.

People who are not honest with each other may try to communicate, but it will be awkward at best and might just fail entirely. If you are not confident that I'm being honest, you'll probably have little interest in listening to what I have to say, and you'll not be moved to share much with me either.

Honesty has powerful implications for our praying.

The psalms teach us that we can talk to God with great freedom. We are free to admit when we are depressed (Psalms 42 and 43) and how troubled we are (Psalm 38). We may tell God when we feel deserted (Psalm 22), when we are lonely (Psalm 25), and when we are haunted by the fact that God seems so silent (Psalm 35). We can tell God when we are frightened by our enemies (Psalm 56), when we feel overwhelmed (Psalms 69 and 88), when we cry ourselves to sleep at night (Psalm 6), and even when we are angry at God (Psalm 13).

But there is another side. Honesty in a vital prayer life must also involve honest confession of our sin. Unless we regularly confess our sins, we cannot claim to pray honestly. And without honest confession, no one will experience the fullness of our new life in Christ. Honesty, confession, forgiveness, and assurance are all part of the same package. Forget the first two and the last two quickly fade away.

Many psalms illustrate this.

David is our primary teacher in honesty. You know his story—adultery with Bathsheba, deceit to conceal it, contrived murder to get rid of her husband . . . followed by silence. David refused to admit it. Not to himself. Not to the prophet Nathan. Not to God. His guilt ate away at him; he was wasting away through his groaning because the hand of God was heavy on him (Psalm 32).

But then the Spirit of God opened his heart to honesty (through Nathan's confrontation), and David confessed. "Have mercy on me, O God, according to your unfailing love; according to your great compassion blot out my transgressions. Wash away all my iniquity and cleanse me from my sin. For I know my transgressions, and my sin is always before me. Against you, you only, have I sinned and done what is evil in your sight; so you are right in your verdict and justified when you judge" (Psalm 51:1-4).

Those words represent honesty and integrity. They represent the genuine confession of a man humbled to the dust before a holy God. But even as he confesses, David is so thoroughly able to trust God that he is confident he will not be destroyed but pardoned.

It's hard to be that honest with other people, even with those nearest to us. And it may be hard to be that honest with God in our praying. But there is no other route to wholeness, to peace, to the renewal that Christ bought for us.

It's a wonderful freedom for me to know I can be honest with God, and I will never be loved less for it. Instead, I'll be pardoned!

Reflecting on God's Word

Psalm 32
Luke 18:9-14
1 Timothy 1:12-17

For Further Reflection

1. In a time of quiet reflection, ask yourself how honest you have been with God. What have you hidden from God? Write it down in a note to God, and then burn it.

2. How much of your personal prayer time is spent on thanks, praise, asking for help, and confessing your sins? Take a close look at these four. Do your prayers reflect a good balance?

3. Look at Psalm 32:1-2: "Blessed are those . . ." Reflect on what that blessedness is and write it in your journal. Look for other words that express it. What does it feel like to you?

9. Others

I suppose it feels natural to focus mostly on ourselves and our needs when we pray because our own needs are the most obvious to us. Human nature is bent toward self-centeredness. Particularly when we experience pain, anxiety, sorrow, and threats, we are easily preoccupied with such concerns and turn inward all the more.

But the psalms give us healthy encouragement to turn our prayers outward, toward others.

In Psalm 72 the focus is not only outward but upward to the king on the throne. This psalm is a prayer for King Solomon, a son of David, who sits on the throne as earthly ruler over God's people. It's a prayer that the king will be able to rule to the honor of God.

"Endow the king with your justice, O God, the royal son with your righteousness. May he judge your people in righteousness, your afflicted ones with justice. . . . May he defend the afflicted among the people and save the children of the needy; may he crush the oppressor. . . . For he will deliver the needy who cry out, the afflicted who have no one to help. He will take pity on the weak and the needy and save the needy from death. He will rescue them from oppression and violence, for precious is their blood in his sight" (Psalm 72:1-2, 4, 12-14)

Psalm 72 a good model for our prayers. The one praying is concerned about God's people in the land and the integrity of the king's rule. But in his heart there's also a vivid picture of others—those who are poor and needy, those who are being oppressed and threatened. In the eye of his heart the psalmist sees all these, and his prayer goes "up" to intercede for the one on the throne in Jerusalem but also "out" to seek help and justice for those who are unprotected and needy.

It goes hand in hand with Paul's advice to Timothy in rich, pagan Ephesus. "I urge, then, first of all, that petitions, prayers, intercession and thanksgiving be made for everyone—for kings and all those in authority, that we may live peaceful and quiet lives in all godliness and holiness" (1 Timothy 2:1-2).

I've had to remind myself of that constantly. It's so easy to pray for ourselves, our needs, our loved ones. But we are also called to pray "up" for kings, rulers, presidents, prime ministers, governors, and all those on every level of government, so that they may carry out the rule of God with fairness, justice, and righteousness. And to pray "out" for the sick, the needy, the poor, the victims of injustice, the oppressed, and the forgotten.

That means the newspaper and the evening news ought to shape our praying. We pray best with a host of vivid and disturbing pictures in our minds.

Reflecting on God's Word

Micah 6:6-8
Luke 4:16-21
Romans 12:9-21

For Further Reflection

1. Take note of how much of your prayers focus on you and those closest to you, and how much focuses on the needs of others in your community and the world. Are you satisfied with what you find? Is it a healthy balance?

2. Now do the same with the prayers in your congregation's worship. How much of the praying is "internal" compared to how much is "external"? Do you consider it to be healthy?

3. This week, pray your way through the newspaper or a newsmagazine. With the stories open on your lap, page through it, note the people referred to, and spend time in prayer for them.

10. Professing

When I was a young boy, I always had the impression that prayer was *asking*. I thought praying is when we ask God for things. So my prayers were riddled with requests, things I needed (or at least things I wanted), and things I thought other people needed. I usually tried to be polite about it, not wanting to sound too demanding. So frequently I said "please" and "we ask that you . . ." to soften it a bit. I guess I didn't like sounding like a rude beggar all the time.

What a stunted view of prayer—and how selfish! If the only time I talked to my parents was when I wanted to ask for something, my home and family life would have been pretty unpleasant.

Fortunately, praying is much more than asking. It is talking to God in the context of all that is important to us in life. Certainly our prayers involve asking—for help, direction, and forgiveness, for others who are in deep need. Our prayers also involve crying to God in fear, pain, and frustration.

But perhaps the dimension of praying that we're most likely to shortchange is simply telling God about our love for him, about what God has done in our lives and how grateful we are for it. If I ask myself how much time I spend in my prayers simply telling God how grateful I am for all he's done, how much I enjoy all of God's good gifts, how much I'm trusting him today and what that means to me . . . I'm forced to admit that I do a lot more asking than anything else.

In contrast, listen to some of the psalmists who shape their prayers around their heart's desire—professing their faith and love toward God. Listen to David in Psalm 40:5: "Many, LORD my God, are the wonders you have done, the things you planned for us. None can compare with you; were I to speak and tell of your deeds, they would be too many to declare."

Listen to him again in Psalm 86:8-10: "Among the gods there is none like you, Lord; no deeds can compare with yours. All the nations you have made will come and worship before you, Lord; they will bring glory to your name. For you are great and do marvelous deeds; you alone are God."

Another psalmist, possibly Solomon, prayed: "My mouth will tell of your righteous deeds, of your saving acts all day long. . . . Since my youth, God, you have taught me, and to this day I declare your marvelous deeds" (Psalm 71:15, 17).

Reading those words makes me feel as if I'm being given the sacred privilege of sitting in on private prayers. I can imagine the prayers lifting up the psalmists' hearts and minds as they cherish the opportunity to tell God directly how much they love him and how rich they feel for having been loved by him.

Today in your prayers, set aside all the asking and just tell God how much he means to you.

Reflecting on God's Word

Psalm 116
Luke 7:36-50
Philippians 3:1-11

For Further Reflection

1. Reflect carefully on the past few years of your life. What do you consider the most significant things God has done for you during that time? Take some time to tell God that you remember those acts and how much you love him for it.

2. Now reflect on all the "little" and easily unnoticed things that God does for you every day. Take your time in this reflection to remember what is so easy to forget. Now take some time to profess to God your love and gratitude for such daily gifts.

3. Write out your profession of gratitude and faith. Write it as a letter to God. Recount God's acts, retrace some of his ways, and profess your love for him.

Living Deeply: Romans 8

My father was a devout Christian man, but in the closing years of his life he struggled with emphysema. Very clearly etched in my memory is the picture of his short breaths, never taken very deeply into his diseased lungs. As a result, the oxygen level in his blood was always either borderline or lower. He was able to engage in only limited physical activities without becoming too exhausted to continue.

Not a pleasant way to live.

Yet many folks live that way spiritually. Their living is shallow because their believing and reflecting is shallow. Preoccupied with things on the surface of life, they never seem to get down to the deep rich values and truths that nourish our spirit for robust living.

The eighth chapter of Romans is a chapter that seems designed for living deeply. It is, frankly, one of the richest chapters of the Bible. Paul, who is deeply in touch with his own spirit and who is pastorally concerned for "deep living" by the Roman Christians, gives them truths that are eternal, promises that nourish their spirits with power, and confidence that leads to vigorous Christian living.

We'll focus on this rich chapter for some time in order to breathe it in deeply.

I suggest that you read the entirety of this mighty chapter each day. Read it slowly, meditatively, and with a lump in your throat.

1. No Condemnation

Condemnation is a frightening thing. It means having a sentence of judgment pronounced against us because of our failures and crimes. In our judicial system it usually involves several stages: indictment, pronouncement of the verdict, sentencing, and the actual implementation of that sentence to carry out the punishment. When Paul uses the word *condemnation*, he's talking about all of those wrapped together.

In Romans 7, Paul explains that this condemnation is the vulnerable natural state of sinners before God. It's the state of being under the judgment of God for our sin. We cannot deny that we were born sinful (see Psalm 51:5) and that we have continued to work that out in our sinful living (see Romans 3:23). No matter how obedient I've tried to be, the fact is I have still "fallen short." If I'm honest, I must admit that I rightly deserve the judgment of God.

But then Paul goes on to say, "Therefore, there is now no condemnation for those who are in Christ Jesus" (Romans 8:1).

No condemnation. That two-letter word is the biggest word of this verse—so strong and prominent that it cancels out everything else that is communicated by the word *condemnation*. It says there's not a single possible chance of any condemnation at all. With that small word, terror is wiped out. Fear is cancelled.

No is the word that paints a picture of the sinner standing before God in colors that are bright and hope-filled. It's the gospel! When you are in Christ, there is no condemnation. It's almost too big an idea to wrap our minds around.

Some Christians are confused about this. They think that Christians keep going back and forth from "condemnation" to "no condemnation" and back to "condemnation" as they fall into sin and confess it and then begin the whole process of sin and confession all over again. They feel as if they are perpetually swinging back and forth from one state to another.

Paul sets us straight. Once we are "in Christ," once Christ has paid the price for our sins and set us free from the law of sin and death, once Christ has satisfied God by his sacrifice, there is only one state for us—no condemnation! It is the state of living before God as one who has been declared innocent by Christ the mediator.

Do I still sin? Yes. Am I still a lot less than God would like me to be? Yes. Does that mean I lose my "no condemnation" status? Absolutely not! Christ's work for me is once and for all, now and forever. I may go back and forth. He doesn't.

The promise of this verse is so big, so eternal, so rich, so deep that I can hardly imagine it. It certainly doesn't fit with what I deserve. But it fits perfectly with the richness of the gospel!

Reflecting on God's Word

Psalm 32
Romans 5:1-11
Hebrews 10:11-18

For Further Reflection

1. What sometimes stands in the way of your assurance of pardon?

2. Are you able to take Romans 8:1 to heart and accept God's Word as true for you?

3. What emotions does this promise evoke in your mind and heart? Try to imagine what it must feel like to hear the pronouncement, "condemned." Now try to imagine what it will be like to hear the final "no condemnation."

2. A Set Mind

The college where I work uses the phrase *Minds in the Making* to describe its mission. It assumes that shaping students' minds well will lead to shaping their lives well, especially for Christians. Occasionally I drive by a billboard sponsored by another college that proclaims, *A Mind Is a Terrible Thing to Waste.*

Both recognize that the mind is a powerful force.

I can still remember my father's voice saying to me, "If you just set your mind to it, you can do it." He knew that our minds have power.

So did the apostle Paul. He said there is a sharp dividing line between two kinds of people, and their mind is what makes the difference: "Those who live according to the sinful nature have their minds set on what that nature desires; but those who live in accordance with the Spirit have their minds set on what the Spirit desires" (Romans 8:5).

Often I wonder why some people stumble from one sinful situation into the next, while others are so productive and seem so noble. At the risk of sounding oversimplistic, I want to say one group sides with God, and the other group sides with our sinful nature.

Just so we don't begin to see this as a human self-help process, let's remember the context in which Paul was speaking. What Paul said at the opening of this chapter lays the foundation for careful mind-setting. If we've been set free from sin and death by Christ (verse 2) and if we now have no condemnation (verse 1), then we are to set our minds on the right things in our new life. We "set our minds" by what we side with, what we are interested in, what we focus on, what we engage in. Paul is saying that Christians have a holy obligation to set their minds right. And we know that God through his Holy Spirit has really set our minds right!

Many Christians seem surprised at how hard this is for them, while at the same time they are absorbing into their minds so much from TV, movies, videos, Internet images, and other sources that directly compete with where their mind ought to be set.

No wonder, then, that Paul speaks so directly about our efforts to renew our minds: "Be transformed by the renewing of your mind" (Romans 12:2). "Be made new in the attitude of your minds" (Ephesians 4:23). "Have the same attitude of mind Christ Jesus had" (Philippians 2:5).

Paul's advice has huge implications for our self-care. If we are redeemed by Christ, then our spiritual growth must involve "minds in the making." If we are new creatures in Christ, then what we feed our minds is of critical importance. If we are parents of children, then what we feed their minds is even far more important than what we feed their bodies.

It's simple. My personal spiritual growth is directly influenced by where and how I set my mind.

Reflecting on God's Word

Jeremiah 31:31-34
Ephesians 5:1-20
Philippians 2:5-11

For Further Reflection

1. What do you think of the fact that our culture today seems to put more emphasis on what we *feel* than on what we *think*? Is that good? Is it dangerous? How can we find a balance of the two?

2. Is it an oversimplification to say "If you set your mind to it, you can do it"? Why or why not?

3. Try to identify four or five healthy ways in which you are feeding your mind today. Then identify four or five unhealthy ways of treating your mind. How can you reinforce the healthy ways and overcome the unhealthy ways?

3. Obligation

*O*bligation is a word with many faces.

It has the face of a seventh-grade boy who knows he must go out to deliver newspapers on a cold day even though he's not eager to do it. And the face of a high schooler who needs to study for her math test. The face of a middle-aged couple still making monthly payments on the mortgage they took out twenty-five years ago. The face of a young girl practicing for her piano lessons. The face of an eighty-two-year-old husband as he lovingly takes care of his wife. The face of a preacher filing this Sunday's sermon away and beginning to prepare for the next one.

It's not a bad word. We all have many obligations in life that need to be faithfully fulfilled.

As Christians, we have a huge obligation—to live a Christian life. "Therefore, brothers and sisters, we have an obligation," says Paul, "but it is not to the sinful nature, to live according to it" (Rom. 8:12).

Notice how the verse begins with *therefore*. This connecting word means that what Paul is saying here is the direct result of what he said just before—that we have no condemnation (verse 1), that we are set free from the law of sin and death (verse 2), that we live according to the Spirit (verse 4), and that the Spirit of God lives in us (verse 8). As a logical conclusion of all of those rich truths, we are now under obligation to live as a new person in Christ.

Paul began this letter to the Romans with his own sense of obligation. Because God has revealed his gospel to Paul, he professes to feel "obligated both to Greeks and non-Greeks, both to the wise and the foolish" (Romans 1:14).

There is something very wholesome about having a clear sense of obligation. The waters of baptism obligated my parents to teach me the ways of the Lord. My baptism placed God's covenant claim on me, and from that day on I have been obligated to live for him. The baptism of my own children gave the same obligations to my wife and me. When I take the bread and the cup at the Lord's table, I am obligated to live gratefully for him. Every time I hear the assurance of forgiveness of my sins, I know I'm obligated to live in thanks.

An obligation (or a debt, as some translations express it) is something that's required of us, something we cannot ignore without being charged with negligence and delinquency. We are morally bound to that duty. The healthy life is made up of faithfully fulfilled obligations.

Many times through the years, my heart has whispered, *I want to go my way; I want it differently; I want to pursue another path; I want to be free to decide myself.* But each time God's voice comes back to remind me of who I am and how I am obligated to him.

And when I resist that whisper to go my own way, when I surrender myself to God's way and to my obligations, then I find the freedom that I really was looking for all the while.

Reflecting on God's Word

Psalm 119:1-16
Luke 19:11-27
Ephesians 4:20-32

For Further Reflection

1. What feelings does the word *obligation* stir up in your mind and heart? Does it carry a negative side to it? Why? How can you correct that?

2. Remind yourself of some Christian practices or opportunities for service that you have been neglecting. Why have you been neglecting them? What can you do to correct that?

3. Ask two or three of your closest friends what Christian disciplines they believe are the most important for their spiritual lives. Ask them whether it is easy or difficult to maintain their obligations. Share with them some of your own experiences.

4. Led by the Spirit

I find it difficult to experience a close bond with someone I cannot see. That's my problem with the Holy Spirit.

I can picture God the Father because I know what fathers are like. And I can picture Christ because he once lived on earth as a young Hebrew man. But the Holy Spirit? How can I picture the third person of the Trinity? When I was a child we always called the Spirit the Holy Ghost, which didn't particularly help.

Even though I can't picture the Holy Spirit, the Spirit is an indispensable and intimate part of my spiritual life. The Bible teaches that the Spirit is the One who brings us to faith in Christ and comforts us and leads us into truth.

In this great chapter of Romans, Paul tells us that "those who are led by the Spirit of God are the children of God" (Romans 8:14). There are two groups of people in that sentence: those who are led by the Spirit and those who are children of God. And they are the same people. No one is part of one group and not part of the other. Children of God are led by the Spirit. Those led by the Spirit are the children of God. Same people.

So I make these two great affirmations about myself: I am a child of God and I am led by the Spirit of God.

When I listen carefully to what Paul says in other epistles, I learn that my relationship with the Holy Spirit is very rich:

- The Holy Spirit has taught me to profess Jesus as Lord (1 Corinthians 12:3).
- The Holy Spirit is always reminding me I am a child of God (Romans 8:16).
- The Holy Spirit lives in me and I am his "temple" (1 Corinthians 3:16).
- The Holy Spirit has sealed me and made me safe in Christ (Ephesians 1:13).
- The Holy Spirit has gifted me (1 Corinthians 12:7).
- The Holy Spirit is producing fruit in me (Galatians 5:22-23).

But I also hear Paul telling me that my relationship with the Holy Spirit is a rather fragile relationship. It's not that I can't always count on the Holy Spirit but rather that the Spirit can't always count on me. Paul wrote to the Galatians, "Since we live by the Spirit, let us keep in step with the Spirit" (Galatians 5:25). That suggests it's also possible for me to get out of step with the Holy Spirit at times.

No wonder Paul has to encourage us to be "filled with the Spirit" (Ephesians 5:18). And surely that's why Paul warns us not to "grieve the Spirit" (Ephesians 4:30) and not to "put out the Spirit's fire" (1 Thessalonians 5:19). He wouldn't say those things if they were not real possibilities.

I may not be able to picture the Holy Spirit, but I know the Spirit is a much bigger part of my life than I often realize.

Reflecting on God's Word

Ezekiel 36:24-28
John 16:5-16
Galatians 5:16-26

For Further Reflection

1. During a time of quiet reflection, repeat the following phrases to yourself multiple times: "I am a child of God—today"; "I am led by the Spirit—today"; "I am sealed in the Spirit—today."

2. In your journal write a list of some of the "gifts" and "fruits" that the Holy Spirit has given you. Then reflect on how you have used those gifts. Look ahead and decide how you plan to use them.

3. Identify times and circumstances in your life when you have "grieved" the Holy Spirit (so that he became sad) or "put out the Spirit's fire" (so that his work in your life was diminished). Confess them and claim Christ's forgiveness.

5. Adopted

Paul considered himself an adopted child of God. The framework of adoption provided the setting for both his sense of privilege and his security. You and I may consider ourselves that way too—we are adopted children of God.

Adoption was a powerful concept in Roman society. Only rarely were infants adopted. More likely an adult, usually an adult son, was installed into the family for the purpose of managing the estate, taking over the family business, and stepping into the wealth and power of the family.

The Robe, a novel by Lloyd C. Douglas, tells the story of seventeen-year-old Marcellus, who has been adopted as the son of a wealthy and powerful Roman family. Writing to a friend about these experiences, he speaks of the elaborate ceremony and the challenge to be absolutely loyal and faithful no matter what. Then he describes the moment when his father put the official white toga on him as a sign of entrance into the family. At that point he felt as though his life had begun.

Adoption is a familiar concept in our society too. Most people know at least someone who was adopted. Two of my grandchildren were adopted from Haiti from situations of poverty and abandonment. For them, adoption isn't merely a legal process, it's a lifeline.

Slaves in Roman society and abandoned children in Haiti both live in fear. Neither have any rights. They are often neglected or abused. They are not sons and daughters but live at the mercy of others.

Those who are adopted have a far different position. They are sons and daughters. They have a loving intimacy with those who care for them. They have a right to nurture, protection, security, and comfort. A right to live free from fear. They have legal and emotional standing in the family circle.

In Romans 8:15, Paul says, "The Spirit you received does not make you slaves, so that you live in fear again; rather, the Spirit you received brought about your adoption to sonship."

I have been adopted—and so have you. Adopted by God. I am secure.

Adoption is an amazing process that is implemented by the Holy Spirit. The Spirit has bound us to God as his children, and the Spirit keeps on reminding our hearts that this is so. The Spirit doesn't ever want us to lose sight of the fact that as God's adopted children we have the right to call God *Abba*, Father, with all the intimacy only a secure child can know.

What's even more amazing is that as adopted children we become heirs—those who stand to inherit an estate. We stand to inherit God's estate. But even more than that, Paul calls us "co-heirs with Christ" (verse 17). That means that everything that is Christ's is ours.

Imagine that!

Reflecting on God's Word

John 1:1-14
Galatians 3:26-4:7
1 John 3:28-4:3

For Further Reflection

1. If you have been adopted into your family, tell them today how much you love them.

2. How does it change your concept of who you are when you know you are adopted by God? What are some of the benefits that you are enjoying today because of your adoption as God's son or daughter?

3. What fears do you have that are unnecessary because of your adoption by God?

6. Groaning and Glory

In my years as a pastor, I've listened to a lot of groaning. Groaning is what we do when our hearts feel pain.

Some parents came to see me and groaned with anguish because their child had left the church. A couple came to tell me their marriage was finished and groaned with profanity toward each other. Another parishioner learned he had cancer, and the whole family groaned. A terrible auto accident happened on a church outing, and the congregation groaned.

As a pastor I've groaned in grief with my parishioners as loved ones passed away. In my own life I've groaned when I had to enter major surgery, when a daughter died, when a son went into surgery. I've groaned when there just seemed too much to handle all at once in my life.

In his letters, Paul is quite honest about his own groaning. He groans about the sad state of the Corinthian church. He groans about the persecution he endured on his journeys. He groans about the thorn in the flesh he had to endure. And he groans about those who were rejecting the gospel of salvation.

Paul hears the Holy Spirit groaning too. The Spirit, who knows our needs and understands our prayers, intercedes for us with groans when we find ourselves in too much pain to pray or too confused to know what to pray for.

If we listen carefully we can even hear creation itself groaning. Creation groans when violent tornadoes level neighborhoods and destroys trees. It groans when hurricanes violate boundaries and flood neighborhoods. It groans when humans pollute streams and kill fish; when ground water is contaminated and becomes undrinkable; when blight or fire destroys beautiful forests.

Groaning is everywhere in our world.

But Paul points to a special kind of groaning: "We know that the whole creation has been groaning *as in the pains of childbirth* right up to the present time" (Romans 8:22).

This is the groaning that accompanies new life. Suddenly, into a dark and groaning world, the hope of new life shines. Even Paul, an unmarried male, knew something of what the pains of childbirth were all about. Intense pains, to be sure, but pains with hope, with anticipation, with the expectancy of new life which would be viewed as well worth it all! There's a kind of groaning that accompanies a redemptive pain that brings new life.

Glory is coming, says Paul. And that glory can't be compared with all the present sufferings that produce all these groans. It's the glory of redemption that is coming, of liberation from all the pain, of the new freedom for which we were originally created. It's "the freedom and glory of the children of God" (verse 21). It's the new creation.

We have this hope. It's ours because we have been adopted and have now no condemnation. Once adopted as sons and daughters, we live with powerful anticipation!

Reflecting on God's Word

Genesis 3:1-20
2 Corinthians 11:16-33
Revelation 21

For Further Reflection

1. Identify your deepest groans right now. What is causing you to feel pain? What pain do you see in others in your congregation? Take time today to reach out and encourage them by phone, text message, or in some other way.

2. Do you think it is legitimate to feel "homesick for heaven"?

3. What do you think the new heaven and new earth will be like?

7. Intercession

Early in my ministry I made a series of pastoral calls on a parishioner after her surgery. It was major surgery, and her recuperation took some time. I knew her to be a very mature and seasoned believer, one whose faith would surely carry her through this time of testing. So I was alarmed one afternoon when she hesitantly admitted to me that ever since her surgery, she hadn't prayed. "I just can't," she said. "I don't know why, but I just can't."

She was dealing with several problems—recuperating from surgery, the loss of her ability to pray, and feelings of great guilt over this. I didn't think it would be helpful to enter a discussion with her about what might be behind this prayerlessness on her part. Instead I reassured her that we'd do her praying for her.

Over the years, in both my pastoral work and my own experience, I've learned that this experience is not unique. At times as a hospital patient I found myself unable to pray. Many of God's children find that at times, for some reason, they can't pray.

When that happens, I've learned that it's best to turn to Romans 8:26-27. Paul puts it this way: "We do not know what we ought to pray for, but the Spirit himself intercedes for us through wordless groans. And he who searches our hearts knows the mind of the Spirit, because the Spirit intercedes for God's people in accordance with the will of God."

There is something wonderfully comforting here. It matters not whether our problem is not knowing what to pray for, or how to pray, or being unable to pray. The point is that there are times when our prayer life stops. And when that happens, the Holy Spirit steps in to deliver us from our difficulties.

The Holy Spirit offers "wordless groans" on our behalf, and the Spirit knows the will of God perfectly while he does that. I'm not sure why they are wordless groans, but I do know that embedded in those prayers is the Holy Spirit's intense love for us. Later in Romans 8, Paul says that Christ also "is at the right hand of God and is also interceding for us" (verse 34). So the Holy Spirit, who lives among us, is interceding for us here on earth, and Christ is interceding for us in heaven.

Add to that the fact that when we're part of the family of God we pray for each other.

We're covered. In fact, we have triple coverage in prayer.

So during those times when, because of weakness, pain, stress, or for whatever reason we lose our ability to pray, we can be guilt-free and still covered in prayer. Christ understands. The Spirit understands. Our fellow Christians understand. They all pick up the task of praying for us.

Reflecting on God's Word

Luke 22:31-32
John 14:15-21
Hebrews 7:23-28

For Further Reflection

1. Recall a time when you found that you were unable to pray. Was it because of confusion (you didn't know what to pray for), or weakness (you had no strength to pray), or was it because you had no motivation to pray? How did you feel at the time? How do you feel about such an experience now?

2. Reflect on the fact that Christ (in heaven) is praying for you right now and the Holy Spirit (here on earth) is doing the same thing. Give thanks for being so "covered."

3. Are you conscious of how other folks have prayed for you at some special time? Think of someone you can do that for.

8. Good Purposes

The teaching of divine election has been a puzzle to many of us. Even the word itself may seem heavy and unappealing.

I believe the Bible teaches divine election, but I also believe Christians have often made it a lot more complicated than it has to be. In Romans 8 Paul talks about a God who foreknew us, predestined us, called us, justified us, and then glorified us (Romans 8:29-30). And he speaks about all five as fully accomplished in the mind of God.

Paul didn't intend to communicate this truth as some deep and heavy doctrine. He was simply explaining to new believers how they came to be Christians. He knew that we are all sinners who can't decide to turn to God by ourselves, and that out of great love for us, God devised a plan for saving us. So Paul went out preaching the Christian gospel, calling people to believe in Jesus Christ. And when they believed, Paul sat down with them and said, "Do you know how it came about that you believed? God loved you and reached out to you long before you were interested in reaching out to him." That's what election means. God loved you, behind the scenes, when you weren't even aware of it.

You can think of this in very personal terms. Have you turned to Jesus Christ for your salvation? But how can that be if you are a sinner who cannot reach out to God all by yourself? The answer is that God has reached out to you first. This is an amazing truth that ought to fill us with awe.

That's one way Paul spoke of what we call the doctrine of election. He takes it to the next step when he uses the doctrine of election to comfort us when events in our lives tempt us to feel like everything is out of control: "And we know that in all things God works for the good of those who love him, who have been called according to his purpose" (Romans 8:28).

Paul reassures us here that God has good purposes and that God is always working toward those good purposes. Those who trust in Jesus Christ can be sure that God is supervising everything in our lives.

Those are the two things the doctrine of election means for Christians. On the other hand, election does *not* mean that we will be protected from pain and suffering. It does *not* mean that everything in our lives will be "good" as we normally define it. There is no quick assurance here that if you love God, all will be well in your life.

Instead there is deep and firm assurance that a higher purpose is always served through all the ups and downs of our lives. Like a beautiful stone that has been shaped by water running over it, God is at work shaping us too.

We know that, Paul says. We know it not because we can calculate it and draw a logical conclusion, but because we trust the God who reached out to us first and wrote down promises like this for us.

The very nature of faith is to rest on the credibility of God.

Reflecting on God's Word

Genesis 50:15-21
Psalm 139
Ephesians 1:3-14

For Further Reflection

1. Reflect personally about what it means that God reached out to you long before you reached out to him.

2. Remember one or two events in your experience that were difficult at the time and since have turned out to have benefits. Perhaps there are other difficult experiences in your life that seem to be bringing no benefit at all. How do you respond to those?

3. Lewis Smedes once said that the deepest believing happens when we "trust God against the grain." What does it take for you to believe or trust God "against the grain" of what is happening in your life?

9. More Than Conquerors

If you've ever done any flying, you've probably had this experience: you board the plane on a dreary, cloudy morning and settle into your cramped seat. There's little to see out the window. The plane roars down the runway and you feel it lift off the ground. Still you see nothing. But after a few minutes, it happens. The nose of the plane cuts right through the banks of clouds and you are suddenly thrust into a whole new world of bright sunshine where all is clear. You can see for miles.

That's what happens as Paul nears the end of his eighth chapter to the Romans.

After Paul spends some time setting forth a great teaching, he often steps back from it, analyzes it, and raises hard questions about it to see if it holds. That's what he does in Romans 8. And then he proceeds to express his firm assurance and conviction. At the end of Romans 8, Paul's firm conviction is this: Christians who often groan, who suffer, can know that they are victorious!

"In all these things," Paul says, "we are more than conquerors through him who loved us" (Romans 8:37).

These words are no pie-in-the-sky effort to deny how hard life can get. Paul has just talked about things like trouble, hardship, persecution, famine, nakedness, danger, and sword (see verse 35)—and he knew about each of these from personal experience. But he comes out of it more convinced than ever that God's adopted children have victory over all of these hardships.

The Romans were well acquainted with the word for *victor* or *conqueror*. The athlete who came out on top in the games earned that title. The general who returned from a successful battle earned it. People eagerly shouted the word while the victor led the parade through the streets of the city. Yet for Paul's purpose, it's just not strong enough. So he expands it to a superlative by adding the prefix *hyper*. Hyper means excessive. We talk about excessive energy or blood pressure that is too high. Paul applies this to Christians: they are no ordinary victors, no victors with a slim margin. No narrow victory pulled out in an overtime battle. They are "hyper-conquerors."

Then Paul pokes around some more to test the firmness of this conviction. Is there anything that can separate us from Christ's love? Could death or life? Could angels or demons or the present or the future or powers or height? Is there anything in all of creation that could possibly erode our firm victory in the love of God in Christ Jesus our Lord? (See verses 38-39.)

These are all rhetorical questions. The answer is a resounding *no*. We are held in such love, our "no condemnation" is so firm, our adoption is so settled, glory will so surely replace our groaning, God's sovereign plan is so secure that we are now, and always will be, "hyper-conquerors" forever.

Reflecting on God's Word

Psalm 91
2 Timothy 4:6-8
Revelation 7:9-17

For Further Reflection

1. What events, influences, or circumstances seem like they will overwhelm you?

2. Write Romans 8:37 on an index card. Then post it on a mirror or near the kitchen sink so you can see it regularly. Memorize it. Then add three or four more of God's biggest promises to sustain you when you need encouragement.

3. Try to find a quiet spot where you can minimize distractions and imagine what God may have in store for you as a hyper-conqueror. Use your imagination to picture what this might be like.

10. No Separation

Sometimes I'm in a very reflective mood. I like the quiet. And then I wonder about things that don't normally cross my mind.

Things like, would I ever come to believe in Christ if it were totally in my own hands? Could I remain faithful to God for my whole life if it were totally up to me? Things like, how can I ever know or imagine what kinds of temptations or doubts or enemies will come my way before I finally leave this earth? And how can I be sure that I will be "safe to the end"?

Is it possible that people who have trusted Christ for their whole life long could be torn away from him just before the end? Do I have to fear that possibility?

There's enough weakness in me and enough enemies of my faith in the world around me that it seems reasonable to entertain that frightening prospect.

That's why my heart treasures the grand conclusion of Roman 8. In no uncertain terms, Paul reassures believers that there is absolutely no possibility that we will be torn away from Christ. There is no room for doubt or fear or insecurity.

Listen to Paul's precious words: "[Nothing] will be able to separate us from the love of God that is in Christ Jesus our Lord" (Romans 8:39).

The chapter ends on that climactic note. But Paul arrives there step by careful step. Gradually he builds to this conclusion with neatly arranged couplets. "Neither death nor life" can do it. "Neither the present nor the future" can separate us. "Nor any powers." "Neither height nor depth" could. And then with one big bold sweep he says, "nor anything else in all creation will be able to separate us from the love of God. . . ."

While Paul has considered these big categories, surely we can read between the lines. My own weakness won't do it; persecution won't do it; oppression and doubt won't; the most intense pain of disease or injury won't. For that matter, even death, the final enemy, has no power over my position in the love of God!

What a firm and powerful testimony!

Paul's testimony has led Reformed Christians to speak about the perseverance of the saints. That doesn't mean we'll be wise enough and strong enough to persevere, but that the love of God that comes to us in Jesus Christ is so deep and strong that no enemy will ever prevail against it. He will keep us!

Those of us who have learned to doubt our own strength find rich comfort in this. And when we look ahead to the closing years of our lives we find rich comfort in this too.

We look away from ourselves and put our trust firmly in God's love in Christ.

Reflecting on God's Word

Genesis 49:29–50:3
Psalm 16
1 Corinthians 15:50-58

For Further Reflection

1. Recall the events of Paul's life. He called himself the chief of sinners and faced terrible opposition and suffering. Read Romans 8:37-39 again against the backdrop of his own experiences.

2. Call to mind some stories you know of Christians who have faced great difficulty and even death, and yet have testified of God's love and faithfulness.

3. Can you begin to imagine (try it!) what it will possibly be like to pass through death and awaken to the awareness that you are now "at home with the Lord"? (See 2 Corinthians 5:8.)

The Seasons of Life

When I was young, I was incapable of (or uninterested in) trying to picture myself as much older. That's true of kids today too. A while ago, speaking with a group of adolescents, I said, "Someday you'll be in my age range and be able to think about your grandchildren." All they could do was snicker. I don't think the snicker was caused by the fact that they didn't care to picture themselves much older, but rather that they were incapable of doing so.

One of the healthy changes that comes with an increase of years is the ability to look at life from a multiple-seasoned perspective.

Looking out my office window, I see the changing colors of the leaves, and at the same time I remember their full green all summer and their buds last spring and bare branches covered with snow last winter. I see one season in light of all four. The season I see now is much richer because I see it in the context of multiple seasons.

In a similar way, as the years add up, we're able to see the present in the light of all the other seasons of life. I live each day well aware of the times when I was a little child, an adolescent trying hard to find my way, a young man working hard to balance all my responsibilities. But sometimes when I look at family albums and the early days captured in those photos, I wonder, Was this really me?

Newspapers often run side-by-side photos of newly married couples and then next to it the same couple marking an anniversary many years later. Despite some faint similarities in appearance, they look so different! Inside they are also different.

We cannot change the march of time. We get older, generally faster than we allow ourselves to expect. Some people are sad as that happens, thinking about all they've lost and left behind. Others tend to get cynical as much of life now seems to pass them by. Still others feel helpless, trying their hardest to stave it off but realizing that they are fighting a losing battle. But we're all much richer and healthier if we accept the present season of life in the context of all the other seasons.

The latter chapters of a book are intended to be more intelligible and meaningful because of the chapters that have gone before. Life is intended to be that way too.

So let's reflect on all the seasons in our "year," all the chapters in our "book." For the most part these will be arranged chronologically. But the reflections on Singleness and Crises are not in chronological order. They may happen at any time.

Happy reading!

1. Precious Beginnings

I don't remember my mother or father ever speaking of her pregnancy with me. Was she well? Excited? Did she feel sick? Were there problems? Was I born on time or early? I only know that I was born at home, as was the custom in those days. Back in those days, people didn't take as many photos as we do today. Certainly there were no ultrasound images.

But I do know from the Bible and from medical science that I existed for approximately nine months before I was born—I was living in my mother's womb.

David had no access to what we'd call scientific or medical information, but, by God's Spirit, he told us what happened there before our birth: "For you created my inmost being; you knit me together in my mother's womb. . . . My frame was not hidden from you when I was made in the secret place. When I was woven together in the depths of the earth, your eyes saw my unformed body" (Psalm 139:13, 15-16).

Medical science verifies what David said about life in our mother's womb. Your doctor can give you an even more detailed description of what was happening there, how it took place, and how intricate it was. You or your children may even have ultrasound images of your "unformed body" pasted in a photo album. And once you were born, your parents and grandparents could see every little detail of your body and even determine which family member you most resembled.

But in Psalm 139, David is not interested in describing the details or stages of pregnancy and birth. Instead he wants to make two things clear. First, this is God's work, and God's creation activity continues through the growth of every new fetus. Second, it's a wonder! The kind of wonder that fills us with awe and amazement and inspires us break out in praise to God the Creator: "I praise you because I am fearfully and wonderfully made; your works are wonderful, I know that full well" (Psalm 139:14).

And it's even more amazing when I consider that God had my whole life planned even while I was in my mother's womb: "All the days ordained for me were written in your book before one of them came to be. How precious to me are your thoughts, God!" (Psalm 139:16-17).

The prophet Jeremiah echoes the psalmist's awe and wonder and rejoices in God's claim on his life: "The word of the LORD came to me, saying, 'Before I formed you in the womb I knew you, before you were born I set you apart . . .'" (Jeremiah 1:4-5).

Think about that. Go back to the beginning—the very beginning—of your own life and look at yourself in those terms. Do the same with your children. And on the days when you can't help but reflect on the inevitable march of time, remember where your life began. It was God's work, and God had his hand on you already before you were born, while you were still in your mother's womb (see Psalm 139:5).

Praise God today for precious beginnings.

Reflecting on God's Word

Genesis 1:26-28
Ecclesiastes 3:1-8
Luke 1:39-45

For Further Reflection

1. If you are a parent, have a conversation with your children (regardless of how old they are) about what it was like and how you felt during the pregnancy that preceded their birth.

2. How does what the Bible says about God's creation of us shape your convictions and actions about the sanctity of life?

3. Get out a photo album with baby pictures of you—better yet, with pictures of your mother during pregnancy. Look at the photos for a little while and reflect that this is really you! Give thanks to God for your mother, and thank God for caring for you through the years.

2. The Joys of Childhood

Let's play a little game of "Remember When."

Do you remember when you first learned to read? When you started school? When you got your first two-wheeler? Where your bedroom was and what it looked like? What sport you played? What successes you experienced? What tough experiences stand out?

Childhood etches memories into our hearts that will never be erased. Some children who are abandoned or abused will never have positive memories. But those with a healthy childhood will have memories packed with joyful things.

Mark's gospel gives us a rare glimpse into Jesus' attitude toward children. While the grown-ups around Jesus thought they were far too busy to pay much attention to "little people," Jesus showed them a different priority. He said, "Let the little children come to me, and do not hinder them, for the kingdom of God belongs to such as these. Truly I tell you, anyone who will not receive the kingdom of God like a little child will never enter it" (Mark 10:14-15).

And then, reinforcing his words with actions, Jesus did something that must have surprised and thrilled all who were watching: "He took the children in his arms, placed his hands on them and blessed them" (Mark 10:16).

Wouldn't it be great to have been one of those children on Jesus' lap? Or one of those parents who saw their very own child sitting with Jesus?

I never wrote a diary when I was a child. But if I had, and if we were to read it together today, I know several joys would come through very clearly.

I was way too young to be aware of the joy of being created in the first place. But gradually it dawned on me that the same person who created all the galaxies and planets created me in my mother's womb. Just think!

And there's the joy of growing. Down in the basement, we always had measuring posts. My dad did, and so did I. Every birthday we'd mark our height on the post. And every year we were so happy to see how much higher this year's mark was compared to last year's. Each year my bones were growing longer, my body was getting bigger. I couldn't understand how that worked, but I could see the evidence that it did.

That growing ushered in the joy of discovery: learning about the world and people and nations and events. In grade school I had to write a report about the banana crop in El Salvador, and though I've never been there, it's a familiar place to me. I know where it is.

But even more important is the joy of being loved. My parents loved me unconditionally. So did my large extended family. Even my siblings did . . . most of the time, at least. And since I was baptized and grew up in a covenant home, I knew my church loved me too. I grew up feeling like one of those kids sitting on Jesus' lap with his hands of blessing on us.

Sure, there were some hard times. My parents often had to deal firmly with my disobedience. But childhood was a time packed with all those joys.

And it went by so very quickly!

Reflecting on God's Word

1 Samuel 3:1-10
Matthew 18:1-7
Luke 2:39-40

For Further Reflection

1. Return to your childhood memories and talk with your siblings and parents, if they're still living, about their memories. Share some of them together. Who were your best friends? What was your most satisfying accomplishment? What was most painful?

2. What are you doing now to create positive and joyful memories in the minds of your children and grandchildren or other children you love?

3. How many young children are part of your church? How does your church makes them feel welcome and blessed? How could you as a congregation do that more effectively?

3. The Search of Adolescence

Some time ago I went to my hometown after having been gone for many years. I drove around looking for familiar landmarks—my school, my friend's house, the creek where we used to go exploring, my old house. I was struck by how many changes had taken place and how much urban deterioration had set in.

The strength of the negative emotions this stirred up took me by surprise. While I have many very positive memories about my childhood, my adolescence feels quite different. On the outside, I suppose, it didn't appear that way. My struggle was all internal: Do I want to believe this or that? Live this way or that way? Follow these friends or those friends? I must have sensed intuitively that so many strategic decisions were being pressed in on me and that I couldn't afford to take them lightly for the sake of my future—although at times I wanted to. It seemed like there were so many contradictory voices calling to me. And all those voices made my adolescence a terribly noisy time.

I wonder how you feel about your own adolescence, whether that was long ago or more recently. Maybe your feelings about it are more positive than mine; maybe you're even surprised to learn that many of us found it so difficult even back then. But no matter how you feel, it's clear that adolescence is decision time—big decisions and little ones, long-term decisions and short-term ones, decisions that can be reversed and those that can't.

There's much to be gained from looking through the rear-view mirror.

In Proverbs 4:1-5, King Solomon identifies how I was steadied during all the noise of that period in my life:

> Listen, my sons, to a father's instruction; pay attention and gain understanding. I give you sound learning, so do not forsake my teaching. For I too was a son to my father, still tender, and cherished by my mother. Then he taught me, and he said to me, "Take hold of my words with all your heart;

keep my commands, and you will live. Get wisdom,
get understanding."

Every time I read that passage I think, There's the dilemma of adolescence! One generation speaking to another with urgent requests to take the right path in the presence of (as he says in the next chapter) strongly appealing contradictory voices. That's why it gets so noisy.

In the middle of all that noise, we often find it hard to remember that God leads us through the advice of other people—people who are imperfect too. As a child I usually followed advice when I got it, but in adolescence I spent a good bit of time sorting through the advice I got before deciding whether or not I wanted to accept it. And sometimes I wasn't so teachable—I knew better, after all!

Even then, faithful, persistent, Christian people loved me for who I was and called me to wisdom. They gave me time to sort things through and were patient when I didn't do that so well.

What's your story?

Reflecting on God's Word

1 Kings 3:1-15
Ecclesiastes 12:1-14
Ephesians 6:1-4

For Further Reflection

1. What kind of reflections do you have about your adolescence? What pleased and challenged you the most? What were your biggest struggles?

2. Who were the most influential people to guide you in trying to determine which of the many "voices" you should listen to? How could you be a positive influence for adolescents you know today?

3. Spend some time, perhaps with a Bible concordance or dictionary, defining what Solomon means by *wisdom*.

4. Parenthood

There is a state of being in the heart of many young couples we could call "the passion for parenthood." It's what leads a young couple not only to desire to spend their lives together, not only to have a baby, but to participate in the shaping of a new generation.

When my wife and I were married, we had that passion. We had conversations about our dream of having children—how many, how soon, and what it would be like. Our three sons had it too when they entered their marriages—clearly anticipating homes with children in them. During my years as a pastor I've observed the same passion in countless young couples.

During pre-marriage counseling, I always insisted that couples tell me some reasons why they wanted to be married—and I told them that "We're in love" is not a sufficient answer. Inevitably those reasons would include raising a family.

"Raising a family" is very different from "having a baby." It's far more comprehensive than simply bringing a child into the world. It includes grooming, shaping, and training children to live productively in the world. For Christians the task of training a new generation takes on even greater significance.

Raising a family involves changing diapers, sitting on the couch reading a book with your kids, teaching them how to ride a two-wheeler, taking them to school, and eventually letting them get behind the wheel of your car to practice driving. It also involves teaching them about God, shaping their faith, and forming in their hearts a Christian view.

If you are a young couple planning your marriage, go ahead and dream. If you are a young parent, you are very busy and probably often weary. If you are a grandparent, you may find great delight in watching your children rise to the challenge of parenthood. If you are a member of a congregation with many children, you probably love to watch them grow. But if you are unmarried or married and wish you could be a parent, you are likely feeling a lot of pain. And if your children have special needs or are sick, you feel the pain like only a parent can.

It's all part of the passion for parenthood, a passion reflected in Scripture:

Samson's parents cried out, "Teach us how to bring up the boy who is to be born" (Judges 13:8).

Hannah exclaimed, "I prayed for this child, and the LORD has granted me what I asked of him" (1 Samuel 1:27).

Solomon exhorted, "Start children off on the way they should go, and even when they are old they will not turn from it" (Proverbs 22:6).

And the apostle John wrote, "I have no greater joy than to hear that my children are walking in the truth" (3 John 4).

Parents are supposed to give their children both roots and wings: roots to go deep, and wings to fly high. In addition to being biological parents, we desire to become our children's spiritual parents. We give them life and do what we can to make sure they grow up strong and healthy. But we are not satisfied with physical growth only. We also want to feed their spirit and set their direction on the way of Christ.

Forming a whole new generation to build the kingdom of God takes a passion that comes from Christ.

Reflecting on God's Word

Exodus 20:12
Job 1:1-5
Acts 16:29-34

For Further Reflection

1. Draw on your childhood memories and remind yourself of the positive influences that shaped you.

2. If you are married, recall your anticipation of marriage and having a family. How did your experiences match your expectations? If you are single or have no children, what role could you play in helping a new generation to build the kingdom of God?

3. If you have friends and family who are grieving because parenthood has become exceptionally painful for them for some reason, spend extra time in prayer for them today and take some steps to encourage them.

5. Singleness and Finding It Good

Those who are single often feel left out when the rest of us are talking about marriage and children. Married folks tend to overlook the fact that single people are a much larger portion of our society and our congregations than we normally realize.

The circumstances of being single are very diverse. Some have never married; others are divorced or are widows or widowers. Some people are content to be single and they prefer to remain so; others hope to be married someday. Some are grieving the failure of their marriage or the death of their spouse. Some single people feel they have found God's will for their lives, some are still searching, and others may be confused.

As a pastor, I've come to realize that the church's emphasis on marriage, covenant, and family has led us to overlook the singles among us far too easily, even if unintentionally. We sometimes forget that all human beings are single at the beginning of their lives, and almost all marriages leave one of the spouses single at the end.

The bias against those who are single is not found in Scripture. "There is a friend who sticks closer than a brother" King Solomon reminds us in the book of Proverbs (18:24).

Jesus, himself single, apparently found that kind of friendship with Mary, Martha, and Lazarus—also single—three people with whom he spent a good bit of his leisure time.

In Mark 3:34-35, Jesus reinforced a significant principle in relationships. When told his mother and brothers were looking for him, Jesus asked a surprising question. "Who are my mother and my brothers?" Then, looking around at all those seated in a circle around him, he said, "Here are my mother and my brothers! Whoever does God's will is my brother and sister and mother."

There is a faith tie between people that supersedes the ties of blood or marriage, Jesus says. No wonder people in the church call each other brothers and sisters! Unfortunately it's a bond that we sometimes fail to acknowledge.

I've seen single people hurt by some of the comments of others in church. And I've seen others hurt because they've felt so overlooked.

Regardless of whether we are married or single, it's important for us to invest in relationships. I can't help wondering if congregations need to do more to care for one another. Many people—perhaps especially single parents—need much more help than our communities normally offer.

We also need to check our attitude toward single people: do we see them as valuable persons who are able to serve in a number of ways even better than the rest of us are because of their singleness, or do we see them as somehow "incomplete"?

Paul envisions the body of Christ this way: "The eye cannot say to the hand, 'I don't need you!' And the head cannot say to the feet, 'I don't need you!' . . . Now you are the body of Christ, and each one of you is a part of it" (1 Corinthians 12:21, 27).

We need each other—young and old, single and married. All are part of the inclusive body of Christ.

Reflecting on God's Word

John 11:1-7; 12:1-3
1 Corinthians 7:25-31
1 Corinthians 12:12-31

For Further Reflection

1. Do you consider singleness to be "less than complete" in some way? Why? How could you be expressing this unintentionally?

2. If you are a single at present, examine how you feel about your single state. Can you see advantages? What are some of the difficulties associated with being single? How can it affect your walk with God?

3. How aware are you of the number of singles in your worshiping congregation? What percentage of the congregation is single—in any of its forms—at present? How should this shape the life and ministry of your congregation?

6. In the Valley of Crises

When we begin a trip we assume that traveling will go well. When we get married we assume the way ahead will be smooth. When we have children we anticipate a rich and rewarding chapter of parenthood. And when we make profession of faith we anticipate receiving all of Christ's blessings. We're wired to anticipate the best—even if that seems a little naive!

Sooner or later we discover that life doesn't always work that way. The journey gets harder than we thought it would; we lose our health; our children get sick; our finances dry up; our marriage flounders; and sometimes we pay a painful price for our faith. As a result many of our dreams are shattered. Tears replace laughter.

I've previously recounted some of the pain and suffering my family has experienced. We've shed tears, known fear, had to give up some of our dreams. Though I love life immensely, it's also been more difficult than I ever thought it would be. No doubt you know that from personal experience too, and you've seen it in your loved ones, your closest friends, and your fellow church members.

The Bible is pretty candid about life's challenges. The Israelites were a covenant nation but they also went into slavery. Jacob was a chosen patriarch but his sons deceived him. David was a man of God but he had many enemies. Mary was blessed to conceive the Messiah but she was told a sword would pierce her soul. Paul was a mighty preacher but he suffered more than we can fathom at the hands of enemies. Millions of believers through the centuries have experienced similar hardships.

We may wince when James says: "Consider it pure joy, my brothers and sisters, whenever you face trials of many kinds, because you know that the testing of your faith develops perseverance" (James 1:2-3). But we know those times do come.

Churches usually have multiple ways of notifying the congregation of those who are in a valley and need our prayers—bulletins, announcements, prayer lines, or email newsletters. Whatever the method, the message is clear: at any given time some of our brothers and sisters are in a time of crisis and need our prayers.

At such "valley times" we need healthy and supportive relationships. Often we'll find great strength and support from our closest circle—our family. But we also need a close support group of trusted friends and a healthy, caring congregation. Those without such supportive relationships find the valleys even darker.

At the same time, we also need quiet times in which we can reflect, pray, sort out our thoughts, and listen to God's promises from his Word. Those private times are more important than ever when valleys come.

The time we spend in "the valley" highlights the need for a healthy faith life that is able to withstand times of testing. Once we're in the valley it's too late to become strong. Our strength comes from cultivating a healthy walk with God over a long period of time.

Such a faith life involves firm belief in the goodness of God and trust that God seeks the best for us always. It also requires a clear belief in God's faithfulness to his promises. At times it takes a willingness to live with the mystery of things that just don't add up. Even then, we trust God, though we may not be able to understand his ways just yet.

Reflecting on God's Word

Psalm 34:1-8
Luke 8:22-25
2 Corinthians 1:3-11

For Further Reflection

1. What has been your deepest valley? How has that tested your faith and your relationship with God? What or who helped you the most at that time? Is that valley past, or are you still in it?

2. Think of someone you know who is experiencing a valley time and is in need of your help and support. In what ways are you able to help?

3. Read the 2 Corinthians 1 passage again. How have you been comforted in your valley times? How has that equipped and enabled you to comfort others in similar valleys?

7. Reassessment Time

Any time of significant change brings the opportunity for reassessment. Entering marriage does that, and so does the arrival of the first child or of disease, divorce, or death. Approaching retirement certainly does.

Today we'll reflect on the time of reassessment that comes when the nest is empty again—the day when the last child goes out the door to enter a new chapter of life. What do you do then—cry, laugh, shout, sigh, ask for your credit card back? All of the above?

When our last son moved out to attend college, it brought changes we were not prepared for. We had taken great delight when his brothers left for college because we sensed they were ready for a new and challenging stage in their lives. But we still had another son at home. Now he was going too! Just the two of us again—the way we'd started out a good many years ago.

Even though we were convinced our youngest son was ready and we were happy for him, our emotions were a strange mixture of excitement at what lay ahead for him, satisfaction in having seen him grow, uncertainty about where the road would lead, relief at how quiet it would be at home now (and how much more space I'd have in the garage), and waves of melancholy as we found out how much we missed him. It may have been an adjustment for him, but it surely was for us too.

New questions pressed in on us. How will we live with just two of us again? Who are we? We've wrapped up so much effort into parenthood, now what? Our finances will be different. The supper table will be different. Home will be much quieter.

This transition time put us in the center of a cultural collision between two life views. One view says all of life, from beginning to end, is to be lived for the honor of God and service to others. So when the nest is empty we need to look for alternate avenues of service. The other view leads us to believe that life is essentially divided into two chapters: the first is for the responsibility of rearing children and tending family and the second is for recreation and rest. It's designed for our enjoyment and pleasure—a reward for having survived the first half. Depending on which view they hold, empty-nesters do their reassessments in radically different ways.

So the very first question is, which view of life will guide us? Will it be the view expressed by the "rich fool" in Luke 12:19: "You have plenty of grain laid up for many years. Take life easy; eat, drink and be merry"? Or will it be the view expressed by Paul in 1 Corinthians 10:31: "So whether you eat or drink or whatever you do, do it all for the glory of God"?

For some the empty nest is a time of having more time, energy and resources to devote to the church and its service to the world. Others are too busy traveling and playing to serve.

Reassessment time will be healthy if the questions we raise come from the Bible rather than from our culture. Let the questions be about what new goals we can establish and what other people or causes we can serve. Let's ask ourselves how we can revel in God's blessings on our "launched" family and how we can communicate our clear testimony at this stage in life.

And then let's move ahead!

Reflecting on God's Word

Psalm 90:7-12
Ecclesiastes 3:9-22
1 Peter 4:7-11

For Further Reflection

1. What preparations are you making for how you will arrange your time, your finances, and your commitments when your children are gone?

2. What has been the most challenging part of preparing your children to step out and begin the next chapter of their lives? How would you assess your children in this regard?

3. Find someone close to you who has been an "empty nester" for some time and ask about his or her experiences. What was difficult? What was challenging? What proved to be most rewarding?

8. Aging

The years add up—and they bring changes.

At first we welcome the accumulation of years. Children can't wait until they are old enough to learn to read or ride their first two-wheeler or earn their driver's license or move out on their own. They eagerly mark their increased height and weight—signs that show they are "growing up." Youth is a time of growth, challenges, new experiences, discovering gifts, and developing abilities in which the potential becomes actual. God's plan seems to gradually unfold. It's a time of great excitement and anticipation.

Next comes a leveling-off period of life. We talk about being "in our prime." We sense that we've discovered who we are, who God wants us to be. Our responsibilities are at a peak. Life is very busy, and we sense that we are at the most productive period in our life. We find that satisfying. We remember those youthful growth spurts and are glad to leave behind all the insecurities that seemed to go along with it. At the same time we try not to think ahead to the time when increasing age creeps up on us. Somehow when we are at our prime, we live with the myth that we can always stay there.

But just as surely as youthfulness turns into middle age, middle age gives way to "senior" time. Our AARP card arrives in the mail and we can get coffee cheaper at McDonald's. Gradually but inevitably the awareness settles in that our lives are fragile and fleeting: in the words of the psalmist, "You have made my days a mere handbreadth; the span of my years is as nothing before you. Everyone is but a breath, even those who seem secure" (Psalm 39:5).

Granted, there is a downside to aging. Our appearance changes, even when we try to resist it. Weaknesses and aches make us more conscious of our bodies. As our physical and mental endurance diminish we search for less demanding schedules. Joints ache, hairlines recede, areas that wre once firm now sag, and we need to turn the TV a bit louder. Slowly we become aware that others' perceptions of us change. At the same time our anxieties tend to rise. Diseases threaten our health. We observe some of the struggles our peers have and wonder about what we will have to face. The rapid changes in our culture begin to baffle us much of the time. In a culture like ours that tends to glorify youth, these changes can be very disconcerting.

No wonder the writer of Ecclesiastes calls these "the days of trouble." No wonder he says, "I find no pleasure in them" (Ecclesiastes 12:1).

At the same time, there is a rich side to aging. Our perspective on life has been seasoned through years of experiences. We are better able to see the big picture of life and the world. We've learned from the past in a way that makes us better able to face the future. Hopefully our faith has deepened. Our confidence in the faithfulness of God is firmer than ever. We may have the privilege and joy of watching grandchildren or our friends' grandchildren grow. And we've experienced so much of human behavior that we can be more patient with others than we used to be.

So the wise seer writes, "Gray hair is a crown of splendor" (Proverbs 16:31). And in Leviticus 19:32, Moses commands the people, "Stand up on the presence of the aged, show respect for the elderly and revere your God."

I like that better now than I did a number of years ago!

Reflecting on God's Word

Psalm 90:1-12
Ecclesiastes 12:1-8
Ephesians 4:11-16

For Further Reflection

1. Some of us are part of the "sandwich generation." We are responsible for caring for our children who are younger and at the same time for our parents who are getting older. What are the challenges of this stage?

2. List five of the gifts and benefits for which you are most grateful as you age. Also think of five concerns you have. How are you making provision for the help you might need?

3. What do you think of the idea, "I've done my part, now I may play"?

9. Dying Well

It's always easier to write and reflect on matters that pertain to living than dying. But every book has a last chapter; every journey has a last mile. And every life has a time of dying. We all know that. And although we generally prefer not to talk about it or even think about it, we cannot escape it.

Becoming acquainted with death happens to all of us in three stages. First, we become acquainted with death *impersonally* when we read or hear about it happening to others. As Scripture teaches, "people are destined to die once" (Hebrews 9:27). Second, we become acquainted with death *interpersonally* when someone in our family or circle of friends dies. The first two stages prepare us for the third stage in which we become acquainted with death *personally*. It happens to us.

I have had conversations with a number of parishioners through the years who knew they were in the process of dying. They exhibited faith that was inspiring, and in their dying they illustrated how mature Christians can grieve. Both of my parents experienced a slow process of dying over a number of years. My father in particular spoke openly about his reflections on dying and how it felt. "I'm not afraid of death," he would say. "Christ took care of that for me." After a quiet pause, he would add, "But I wonder what the process of dying will be like." He took great comfort in the words of Psalm 23: "Even though I walk through the darkest valley, I will fear no evil, for you are with me. . . ."

My father taught me about dying well. Unfortunately, those whose deaths are sudden and unexpected never have the opportunity to exhibit their faith by dying well.

Scripture also includes examples of dying well. Abraham and his grandson Jacob are two such examples, and perhaps that is why their deaths are recorded in some detail in the Bible in the book of Genesis. "Abraham lived a hundred and seventy five years. Then Abraham breathed his last and died at a good old age, an old man and full of years; and he was gathered to his people" (Genesis 25:7-8). Similarly, "when Jacob had finished giving instructions to his sons, he drew his feet up into the bed, breathed his last and was gathered to his people" (Genesis 49:33).

These accounts point to a number of ingredients that a "good death" will involve. Such a death takes place within a family circle where folks accept its reality and do not hide from it. Meaningful conversations take place; lifelong instructions are reinforced. The death comes after a long life "full of years"—full not only in number but in richness. And it happens in the context of hope—the confidence of an after-life in which they will be "gathered to their people." I'm convinced that those words are more than merely a reference to where Abraham and Jacob were buried. They are one of the earliest revelations from the Old Testament that the church of God is an eternal family, and we are all united after this life.

None of us knows the details of our death. We don't know when we'll die, or how slowly. But we may pray for the opportunity to have a good death.

What would that look like for you?

Reflecting on God's Word

Psalm 23
John 11:25-27
Hebrews 9:27-28

For Further Reflection

1. As a Christian, examine your thoughts and feelings about dying. How often do you think of it? What do you fear? What hopes do you have?

2. Recall some of the deaths in your family or acquaintances. What were they like? What precious memories did you carry with you? What do you wish had been different?

3. Have you considered making preparations for your time of death (no matter what your age)? Are your legal and financial matters in order? Do you have a will? Have you expressed and written down your preferences for your funeral? Have you talked about this with loved ones?

10. Finally at Home

This section could not end with the previous devotional. After all, "dying well" is not the last word. For that matter, death is not the last word. It's only one more transition that we go through on our way to experiencing the fullness Christ came to provide for us.

Some years ago an uncle of mine died very suddenly and unexpectedly from a heart attack. He was a preacher in his fifties. When his family returned home from the hospital they found a half-written sermon on his desk. It was entitled "Citizens of Heaven" and was based on Philippians 3:20: "Our citizenship is in heaven. . . ." That sermon served as a declaration that we should not speak of death as the last word for him. Instead we understood that he was finally at home.

The fact that we can speak about finally being at home after our death completely changes our understanding of the power of death and dying. Death is an enemy, something we fight with all our strength, but when it comes, a new beginning happens.

Listen to some of Jesus' startling words about life and death from John's gospel:

- "Whoever believes in the Son has eternal life . . ." (3:36).
- "Very truly I tell you, whoever obeys my word will never see death" (8:51).
- "My sheep listen to my voice; I know them, and they follow me. I give them eternal life, and they shall never perish . . ." (10:27-28).
- "I am the resurrection and the life. Anyone who believes in me will live, even though they die; and whoever lives by believing in me will never die" (11:25-26).

No one has ever spoken more amazing words than that! We *have* (present tense) eternal life. We will never really see death. Jesus gives us eternal life. We will live even though we die. And if we live and believe in him, we will never die.

Even though our physical body may have to go through a process of ceasing to exist, we will continue to live in a new, glorified, perfected state. Call it what you will—heaven, eternity, glory, paradise, home—we will not pass out of existence. And this new "at home" state will include all the perfections of glory that Christ has purchased for us.

Many have offered fanciful and imaginative descriptions of what happens, but I believe we must be content in knowing what the Bible teaches. It will certainly involve being at home with the Lord immediately (2 Corinthians 5:8), our full citizenship in heaven (Philippians 3:20), our participation in the final return of Jesus Christ (1 Thessalonians 4:16-17), the eventual resurrection of our body when Christ returns (1 Corinthians 15:51-52), participation in the entire glorified church (Revelation 7:9-10), a renewed creation (2 Peter 3:12-13), freedom from all sin, pain, and imperfection (Revelation 21:1-5), and participation in the reign of Christ (Revelation 22:5).

When my father was dying, I asked him what he thought it would be like when he got there. He was quiet for a while, and then he said, "Eye has not seen, ear has not heard. . . ." And then he would say no more.

That is enough for me. It will be the ultimate surprise.

Reflecting on God's Word

2 Corinthians 5:1-10
Revelation 4 and 5
Revelation 22:1-6

For Further Reflection

1. "Whoever lives by believing in me will never die" (John 11:26). How are we to understand Jesus' words when we stand by the casket of a loved one?

2. Does your view of the resurrection and eternal life influence your choice of embalming or cremation or other funeral practices?

3. After reading Revelation 4 and 5, make a list of the most outstanding experiences that you think heaven will involve.

When It's Cloudy

Most of us, at least those of us in the Western middle class, are somewhat surprised when life gets difficult and clouds roll over our lives. We seem to think we are entitled to sunshine most of the time. Those of us who've lived in Michigan have had to learn that, though we usually have gorgeous sunny summers, we get more than our share of gray, cloudy weather for the rest of the year.

Like many people, I find that those long cloudy spells can cause a pervasive sadness to sweep over my moods. There's even a name for it: Seasonal Affective Disorder. It's not terribly serious and it doesn't affect my ability to function, but I can't help noticing that a bright sunny day makes me feel like a very different person.

I've found that to be true in ministry too. Many of the experiences in ministry are bright, cheerful, inspiring, and uplifting. We see people grow, deepen, and make good decisions. We see them get baptized, profess their faith, and work in God's kingdom. But there's a cloudy side too—not only our own weariness but also the doubts, disobedience, diseases, and dissension that run through the body of Christ.

And I've experienced it in my own life. I've seen God's good care in providing me with more sunshine than I expected. Day after day God has poured out his mercies and favor. I've tried to identify God's grace in these devotionals. But I wasn't prepared for the clouds that would also come. I should have known better because my mother was in debilitating pain nearly all her adult life and had to deal with the depression that came with that. My daughter died at birth, one son has had several critical surgeries, and my three-times encounter with cancer pretty well rocked me to the core. Seasons of sadness, weariness, and discouragement often seemed to dog me.

At school and in church we used to sing an old gospel hymn called "Trust and Obey." But experience has shown me that one of the verses we sang simply isn't true: "Not a shadow can rise, not a cloud in the skies, but his smile quickly drives it away. . . ."

Those clouds and shadows don't quickly fade away. Sometimes they linger far longer than we can easily cope with. Some of the clouds are long-lasting. Many of us struggle hard with why the clouds don't lift quickly.

In this section, let's reflect together on how trust can help us deal with clouds that come . . . and stay.

1. Wounds

The world inflicts wounds on us. No doubt you've had your share of those experiences. Healthy living requires some way to cope with and hopefully resolve these wounds.

Wounds come in many different sizes, shapes, and degrees of severity, and they come from different sources. Some are physical. They're the result of injuries, surgeries, attacks, and disease. Some are inflicted intentionally; others are accidental.

Other wounds are emotional. These arise from the stresses of life, crises we face, sorrow and grief, anger and bitterness. Some of these wounds come from people who have said and done things that hurt us, intentionally or otherwise. These wounds are less visible and much more difficult to resolve.

Still other wounds are relational. People we have counted on for support let us down. People who vowed to be with us desert us. One-time friends seem to have become enemies. Family members have turned on each other. The courts are filled with instances of family brokenness that have degenerated into outright abuse. Broken relationships are a twisted thread woven all through the fabric of society.

But the most difficult wounds to handle are spiritual. We count on fellow Christians for care and support, but when they turn against us we find it hard to trust anyone anymore. When the church, which is supposed to nurture and care for us, mistreats us instead, we lose our security. When life is hard and seems unfair, we are tempted to feel that God has let us down. When we sincerely offer our prayers for help but nothing seems to happen, our disappointment becomes a wound more painful than a physical blow.

All of us have wounds of one kind or another. Some of these wounds we're very conscious of; others slowly and steadily do their harm and inflict their pain just below the level of our consciousness.

In a society that bears so many wounds, the church of Jesus Christ has a more important role than we may have realized. One of the tasks of the church is to faithfully proclaim the good news of God the

Healer, the One who meets us in all our wounds, a gospel proclaimed throughout the Old and New Testaments:

- "[The Lord] heals the brokenhearted and binds up their wounds" (Psalm 147:3).
- "The power of the Lord was with Jesus to heal the sick" (Luke 5:17).
- "At that very time Jesus cured many who had diseases, sicknesses and evil spirits, and gave sight to many who were blind" (Luke 7:21).
- "On each side of the river stood the tree of life . . . and the leaves of the tree are for the healing of the nations" (Revelation 22:2).

The Bible closes with this picture in Revelation of the New Jerusalem with the river of the water of life flowing through the city. Yet while I hold before myself and all others this picture of God the Healer, it saddens me that so many of us in the church are dealing with so many wounds.

It must sadden God the Healer too.

Reflecting on God's Word

Malachi 4:1-6
Matthew 18:1-9
Ephesians 4:25-32

For Further Reflection

1. Look back in your life. When and from what has God healed you? How have you expressed your gratitude?

2. Are there wounds that you have inflicted on someone for which you have never asked forgiveness? Are there others whom you need to forgive for wounding you?

3. Who do you know who is wounded and could use some words and gestures of encouragement from you today?

2. Dis-ease

Most of the clouds I've experienced have been associated with my body. Good health is not only very enjoyable; it also enables me to lead a productive life. And therefore the loss of good health creates a sense of dis-ease. When I lose the gift of good health, the clouds roll in and I get down.

I was ordained to the Christian ministry in September 1962, and was looking forward with great anticipation to a lifetime of service. Two months later I was hospitalized with a hemorrhaging ulcer. As a result, I spent the first Thanksgiving of my ministry in the hospital sipping Cream of Wheat! I felt the pain of being unable to lead my congregation in Thanksgiving worship. But an even greater pain came from the self-doubts and dis-ease that made me ask myself, "What's the matter? Can't I handle life in the ministry?" Sensing my discouragement, a relative who also happens to be a minister, wrote me a very encouraging letter reminding me that sometimes "lying between the white sheets" can be the best preparation for ministry to people.

That hospital stay was only the first of many more. Ten years after that first hospital stay, in 1972, I was diagnosed with lymphoma. Surgery and treatments followed the diagnosis. The dis-ease was not associated with physical pain so much as it was with the fear of having both my life and my ministry cut short. The same thing happened in 1984 when cancer appeared again. And then once more in 1990.

My body seemed to be plotting against my desire for a healthy life of service. I wondered at times whether forces within my body were determined to sabotage my love for life. Was my body becoming my enemy? In addition to disease, I experienced times of nagging fatigue, weakness, and weariness that sapped my spirits.

And so the clouds rolled over the landscape of my life. They weren't really storm clouds, the kind that make you fear a disaster is pending. Not the kind that produces lightning that may strike at any time. They were like the gray clouds of a Michigan winter—hanging low, always just there, day in and day out, blocking or at least diluting the sunshine we long to feel on our faces.

Those were the times when I could identify closely with the psalmist: "Why, my soul, are you downcast? Why so disturbed with in me? Put your hope in God, for I will yet praise him, my Savior and my God" (Psalm 42:11; 43:5).

I came to realize that when my spirit sagged, it wasn't first of all a problem with my spirit but with my body. While God had wonderfully created my fully formed body, that very body seemed determined at times to sabotage the life of service I wanted so much. I am amazed, therefore, at people like John Calvin, who could live such a productive life even when his health was so poor.

I've found it somewhat freeing to realize that my cloudiness was not so much a spiritual problem as a physical problem. I am a whole person, and my body and spirit interact with each other constantly.

Put your hope in God, says the psalmist, for I will yet praise him.

Reflecting on God's Word

Psalm 139:13-18
1 Corinthians 6:12-20
Philippians 1:19-26

For Further Reflection

1. Think back to a time when you had a severe cold or the flu. Why do you suppose it is so difficult to feel inspired spiritually when you feel sick?

2. Reflect on the connection between the health of our body—or lack of it—and the outlook of our spirit. What does this say about the care of your physical health?

3. In the light of the previous question, reflect on God's act of giving us a Sabbath and calling us to keep it holy. Why is Sabbath-keeping important for our health?

3. When We're Weary

Everyone knows what it feels like to be weary. It happens in the normal course of events, and so God planned a night of rest into every twenty-four-hour period and a Sabbath into every seven-day week.

Sometimes, however, weariness becomes more than normal fatigue. Such weariness may be located in our body, in our mind, or in our spirit.

Parents know the deep-down weariness of trying to keep up with the activities of young children, especially when they are sick. Teachers feel it after a full day in the classroom. People who work the night shift sometimes find that their body clocks become disoriented.

And there's a special kind of weariness that people in the caring professions experience. I was naïve about that when I entered the ministry.

First was the incessant list of tasks to be fulfilled. Two sermons to write for each Sunday, agendas and reports to finish, appointments to keep, calls to make and return, meetings to attend, books to read, and visits to make to parishioners in hospitals and nursing homes. There was always more to do. The day was never long enough. Soon it became overwhelming.

But an even greater danger for those in the "helping" professions is what's called "compassion fatigue." A pastor cares deeply for so many people who are in need that he or she can get to the point where it's hard to care anymore. Doctors and nurses experience the same thing. The apostle Paul addresses compassion fatigue in his letter to the Galatians: "Let us not become weary in doing good, for at the proper time we will reap a harvest if we do not give up" (6:9).

For years that verse evoked a strange ambivalence in me. On the one hand I found strange comfort in it because Paul was admitting that doing good produces its own kind of weariness. He knew that. Obviously the Galatians knew it too. On the other hand, the verse frustrated me because I wanted to shout back, "Great—now just tell me how *not* to 'become weary'!" Paul seemed to be saying, "Keep on and never give up, no matter how weary you get." I felt like he was telling me that doing good is so important that our weariness must never stand in the way. But then, won't the weariness just get deeper and deeper?

I spent years wrestling with that, trying somehow to integrate my fatigue into my intensity in ministry. I never have fully resolved it, but I've learned two directives from Scripture that have helped me.

The first is to remember where my real strength lies. It doesn't come from within me—I run low far too quickly. My strength comes from the Lord, who, Paul says, "will meet all [my] needs according to the riches of his glory in Christ Jesus" (Philippians 4:19). I need to remind myself that my strength is insufficient; I will fail if I trust in my own strength. Instead I must constantly draw on God's strength.

The second directive is about our need for Sabbath time. Those of us who are accustomed to being on the job on Sunday need to realize that this command is for us too. We must find other times away from the pressures of work to renew ourselves, to reflect, to rest in God.

Working in God's kingdom, whatever we do, requires a stewardship of our health and resources.

Every one of God's servants finds that out.

Reflecting on God's Word

Isaiah 40:25-31
Luke 6:12-16
Hebrews 12:1-3

For Further Reflection

1. Try to identify how you may be experiencing "compassion fatigue." How might the principles of trusting in God's strength and Sabbath rest help you to address it in your life?

2. Why is it so tempting for us to attempt to do God's work in our own strength? How much of this is behind the weariness you experience?

3. Think about your pastor and the multiple duties she or he carries. Do you see signs of dangerous weariness? Pray for your pastor and send a note of encouragement.

4. Unbelief

I've always considered myself to be firm in my faith. Aside from wondering occasionally whether there could be any possibility that the Christian faith would someday be discovered to be a hoax, I never seriously doubted. When my parents taught me what to believe, I accepted it readily. When my church instructed me further in the truths of the Christian faith, I didn't resist those truths at all. Willingly I made a public profession of faith during my adolescence.

Later I began my ministry with the full confidence that I could spend a lifetime preaching and teaching these truths to others.

But when cancer came, I learned much more about myself. One of the surprising things I learned is that there's some unbelief rumbling around in my heart just waiting for a place to land. I hadn't expected that. The discovery brought with it some cloudy days.

Some unwelcome questions began whirling around in my head. Questions like, Does God really take care of his children as well as I've said he does? Is God really able to heal hurts the way I've claimed God can? Does God heal diseases? Does he really pay attention to every prayer that we send to him?

I was disappointed in my own heart for raising these potentially strangling questions marks. But I realized that many experiences in my pastoral work of sitting with suffering parishioners had brought up these same questions, even though I had quickly repressed them.

And then one day I read the story in Mark 9 about the father of the boy possessed by an evil spirit. At that time I was the father of three young boys, so it was natural that I identified easily with this father. I wondered how I would feel if one of my sons was so afflicted. Would I bypass the ineffective disciples and go directly to Jesus? I felt a little nervous when Jesus seemed to push the father a little and said, "If you can? Everything is possible for one who believes."

But it was the father's statement in verse 24 that really caught my attention: "I do believe; help me overcome my unbelief!" (Mark 9:24).

A light went on then. That was exactly it! It wasn't so much that I didn't believe, but right alongside my belief, in uncomfortable proximity, was this "unbelief" that made me ask hard questions I had never seriously asked before. What a huge admission by the father in this story to acknowledge that both belief and unbelief existed side by side within his heart!

What freedom for me to acknowledge that I was the same!

Jesus seems to have no discomfort with this. He has no words of rebuke for the father. He proceeds with actions that seem designed to bolster the man's belief and destroy his unbelief.

It was one of those "aha!" moments in which one of life's big struggles suddenly becomes very clear. The life of faith involves admitting that belief and unbelief are side by side within our hearts, and then deliberately engaging in spiritual disciplines that can strengthen the belief and starve the unbelief.

Whether we are recuperating ourselves or calling on a parishioner or writing a sermon or addressing a crisis of mind or body or relationship, the task is the same—to strengthen belief and starve unbelief.

Reflecting on God's Word

Psalm 37:1-7
Mark 2:1-12
2 Timothy 3:10-17

For Further Reflection

1. Read the full story in Mark 9 and write down what you think the father was saying to Jesus. Have you ever said anything similar to Jesus?

2. Are you free to admit to others what things stir your unbelief?

3. What are some of the faith-builders (spiritual disciplines) in your life that help to strengthen your faith?

5. The Silence of God

Preachers are generally recognized as people who speak for God. They are expected to fill the prophetic office and pass God's truth on to others. So they go to school for a long time to study and prepare, and they keep on examining the Scriptures so they can preach God's message Sunday after Sunday. Most people assume that preachers live close enough to God—at least most of the time—to be in a position to speak for God. That makes it a fascinating calling, though mighty intimidating—people often expect you to have a word from God for any and all situations they may bring, even terribly complex and long-standing family and personal problems.

It's true that preachers are called to fill the role of prophet. As Paul said to the Romans: "How can they believe in the one of whom they have not heard? And how can they hear without someone preaching to them?" (Romans 10:14). All well and good. The preacher must know the mind of God and the Word of God. Otherwise she or he has nothing to say that's reliable and true.

But what happens when the preacher finds that God doesn't seem to be saying much? God's Word is always there for us, of course. But there are so many other questions and needs for which we seek a good word from the Lord. Sometimes God speaks, but often he doesn't. When that happens we feel as if we are living in the days of Eli and Samuel.

I used to get stuck on this verse from 1 Samuel: "In those days the word of the LORD was rare; there were not many visions" (3:1). I would ask for some help and it didn't seem to come. I'd raise my questions with God and get no answers. I'd beg for him to resolve some troublesome situation and nothing happened. God was silent.

And then gray clouds rolled over the landscape of my heart again.

My questions usually came out of my pastoral work. I'd join a young couple in crying out to God about their infertility and beg for a pregnancy, but nothing happened. I'd sit with a husband and wife who wanted to kill each other and beg for solutions, but none came.

I'd agonize with parents over a son who'd left the faith, but God never seemed to hear our cry. I'd pray for healing and parishioners would die. I'd ask God to take others soon because they were so ready, but still they lingered in that vague land between life and death. I'd call on God to open some new doors for service, but that didn't happen. So what was I supposed to do?

Many other leaders have felt the same way. One psalmist complained: "Why, LORD, do you stand far off? Why do you hide yourself in times of trouble?" (Psalm 10:1). David cries out: "How long, LORD? Will you forget me forever? How long will you hide your face from me?" (Psalm 13:1). I'm in familiar company when I wrestle with the silence of God. But that doesn't solve my problem.

I've come to understand that there is no real solution to the silence of God. There is only trust.

So I will trust God though I do not hear him right now. I will trust that God is on the throne. I will trust that God has our good in mind. I will trust that God has not forgotten us. I will trust that God is not hiding. What's more, I will trust that God has already told me everything I need to know right now in his written Word.

Yes, I will trust that God is up to something big, something good.

Reflecting on God's Word

Psalm 34
Psalm 37
Psalm 116

For Further Reflection

1. Think of friends or family members who are going through a time in which God seems to be silent. Pray for their faith to hold firm, and then encourage them with a word or note.

2. Remind yourself of a time when the silence of God was a burden to you. What did you do? What helped the most?

3. Looking back, how are you able to see how God was at work even though you did not recognize it at the time? What can you learn from that?

6. Unfair!

Life is unfair. That's a charge made by countless voices, and I've heard it from many of them:

- From a businessman who worked hard all his life under a lot of stress, always aiming for the time he would retire and have time to travel and enjoy himself. At sixty-five he retired. Three weeks later he suffered a debilitating stroke. . . .
- From Christian parents who loved their daughter dearly and tried their best to train her in the Christian faith. She was a model daughter until at age eighteen she rebelled and put them through what no parent ought to go through. . . .
- From a young couple, deeply in love with each other and eager to begin their family, who found out that infertility would block that dream. . . .
- From the parents of a three-year-old girl who brought joy to her parents and life to the entire neighborhood until one day she struck down and killed by a drunk driver who hit her on the sidewalk. . . .

I've said those words myself. Why should my daughter die when we wanted her so much? Why should I get cancer when my life was devoted to serving God? Why more than once? And why should all these faithful, God-loving parishioners and friends of mine be struck with every manner of illness, tragedy, and heartache? Why should Christian ministry involve caring for so many good people who, for no apparent reason, suffer terribly painful experiences?

There are no easy answers or ready explanations.

I had to learn that. Early on, as an eager young pastor, I assumed that I had the answers to all of life's questions, answers that should satisfy the complaints of all the sufferers. I spoke my easy answers far too readily—until I entered my own crucible of suffering. And then, when others tried to speak the same easy answers to me, I found those answers didn't help. Not only did they fail to help but they increased my pain and sometimes made me angry. All those glib answers reminded me of the Teacher's oft-repeated comment "Meaningless! Meaningless! . . . Utterly meaningless! Everything is meaningless!" (Ecclesiastes 1:2).

No clouds are darker than the clouds that come when life seems to make no sense, when it all seems so unfair.

I searched, as others have searched, while under those dark clouds. I never did find answers. But my search led me to several other profound truths for living. I learned that trust in God is my calling, trusting God even when everything seems to shout the opposite. I learned that I have God's Word, packed with his promises, which he proves over and over again. I learned that Jesus walks with his arm around my shoulder, even weeping with me; he fully understands all my stirred-up emotions. And I learned that there is a perfect world coming for us through the victory of Jesus Christ.

I still don't have all the answers to those big questions. Even so, I can hold on . . . and trust God.

Reflecting on God's Word

Psalm 34
Ecclesiastes 12:9-14
Luke 8:22-25

For Further Reflection

1. What are some of the different ways and motives in which to ask God why? Are some more acceptable than others? Why or why not?

2. When Jesus asked the disciples in the storm, "Where is your faith?" what do you think he was expecting them to say or do? What would you have done?

3. How would you help someone who is on the verge of becoming very cynical about the fact that life at times seems so unfair?

7. Messiness in Church

The church of Christ can be a very messy place. A lot messier than I thought when I first agreed to serve in the church. Doesn't the Bible describe the body of Christ the place where people love each other, love the Lord, and work together in unity?

So it was a mighty rude awakening when I left seminary and set out to serve the church. My idealism was quickly smashed when I learned that sometimes embarrassing stories about church members had to be discussed at an elders' meeting; when some members refused to speak to each other and still assumed they could show up at a communion service; when I overheard some of the vindictive things people said to each other in church meetings; and when I discovered that even I as a pastor was not immune to painful attacks. I married people but later saw them divorce. I baptized children who later left the faith. I led church meetings in which people behaved in ways that kept me awake at night.

So much for the beautiful bride of Christ! Coming to that realization was pretty disillusioning. Sometimes it made me angry, other times just very sad.

Gradually I came to realize that I had only studied and thought about one side of the church. I'd focused on the church as the bride of Christ, on the church triumphant and the church militant, the church as organization and as organism, the church as custodian of the sacraments.

But there is another side. The church is a gathering of sinners who are forgiven by the grace of God but still have to overcome their pattern of living sinfully. With that realization I began to read the Bible with eyes open for the "other side" of the church.

Moses' frustration and fear in the wilderness helped to open up this "other side." After God's people were miraculously delivered from Egypt, led through the Red Sea, and fed with manna each morning, how did they behave? They grumbled and quarreled because they couldn't get the kind of fresh water they wanted. They questioned why Moses had even led them out of Egypt. Moses was so frustrated that he cried out to God, "What am I to do with these people? They are almost ready to stone me" (Exodus 17:4).

Paul was no stranger to that kind of frustration either. Corinth was the church that he loved dearly but also wept over. He lay awake nights worrying about all the messiness in the life of this congregation: divisions, quarreling, jealousy, arguing, polarization, immorality, lawsuits, and more—just read the first six chapters of 1 Corinthians. No wonder he tells them, "I could not address you as spiritual but as worldly—mere infants in Christ. . . . For since there is jealousy and quarreling among you, are you not worldly? Are you not acting like mere human beings?" (1 Corinthians 3:1, 3).

I had to remind myself that I had not made profession of faith to join a perfect church. I had not taken vows of ordination to serve a sanctified church. Instead I took up my role of leadership in the church to be a shepherd and caregiver for the body of Christ that is still "on the way"—not yet all she's supposed to be, but on the way.

Participation in the church of Christ takes patience, forgiveness, forbearance, and constant trust in the grace of God that is still willing to wrap us in Christ's love.

Even while we are sinners.

Reflecting on God's Word

Isaiah 1:1-20
Ephesians 4:1-6
Revelation 7:9-17

For Further Reflection

1. "Christians aren't perfect, just forgiven." Is that bumper sticker slogan a good way to express life in the church, or can it be misleading?

2. In Ephesians 4:2, Paul counsels Christians to be humble, gentle, patient, "bearing with one another in love." How would that work out in a local congregation? What difference would it make in your church?

3. What do you think is the greater danger in the church today—to be too judgmental toward each other or too forbearing toward each other?

8. Aimless

Ever since fourth grade I had my mind set on being a preacher. All the way through grade school, high school, and into college that dream remained alive. Only briefly did I go through a time of questioning and glancing in other directions, times that were necessary in order to verify my original dream. I know that's not the usual pattern with most folks.

Some people experience a haunting kind of aimlessness in life.

A young man came in for a conversation with his school counselor. He was caught in the cloudiness of life that aimlessness produces. He knew very well that a good stretch of years lay ahead of him, and he felt the pressure of realizing that the choice of what to do was his. No one would make the choices for him. He also sensed that if he chose wrongly or foolishly he could be headed down a long road of unhappiness and wasted years.

When the counselor asked, "What would you like to do with your life?" he responded, "I have no idea." To the question "What interests you the most?" the young man replied, "I really don't have a clue." His counselor tried another approach. "What can you picture yourself doing ten years from now?" "I really don't know," was the persistent and monotonous response, each time spoken while staring down at the floor. Life was a big puzzle, and he couldn't find the pieces.

For people with no sense of direction, cloudiness is a constant companion. How can anyone love life and find it fulfilling if there is a total absence of goals? How can anyone find deep motivation for living if the puzzle doesn't have all the pieces?

Sometimes we can see much more clearly through a rearview mirror. I'm grateful that I can see God's hand on me from the beginning. I see God gently guiding, steering, correcting, protecting, and stretching me through the years. My life is a story of his faithful leading—a story of grace.

But more and more it has also become something else. It is a story not only of deep gratitude but also of great relief—gratitude because

God gave me what I didn't deserve; and relief because he rescued me from a life of aimlessness.

In his letters, Paul expressed some deep theological truths and some great mysteries of faith. But he also said some very personal things that allow us a peek into his heart. Several times Paul called himself an apostle. But three times he described himself as a *servant* of Jesus Christ—at the beginning of his letters to the Romans, to the Philippians, and to Titus (Romans 1:1; Philippians 1:1; Titus 1:1).

There is enough content packed into that word to permanently erase any cloud-producing aimlessness in life. It's a strong word. It describes someone who is totally owned, twenty-four hours a day, seven days a week, to fulfill the Master's purposes.

Nothing chases away the clouds of life like living as servants of Jesus Christ.

Reflecting on God's Word

1 Samuel 3:1-10
Matthew 20:20-28
Romans 6:1-14

For Further Reflection

1. The word *servant* in Paul's letters is often translated "slave." Use a Bible dictionary to determine what this word meant to Paul's hearers. Where would it be used today?

2. In Matthew 20:27, Jesus said, "Whoever wants to be first must be your slave." What do you think he meant?

3. In John 13, after Jesus had washed the disciples' feet, he said, "I have set you an example that you should do as I have done for you" (verse 15). What did he mean for us, and how does it shape our aim in living?

9. Darkness

Psalms of lament make many of us feel uneasy. Either we admit our discomfort with them and wish they had never been included, or we conveniently ignore them without comment or thought. Psalms ought to be filled with praise, teaching, wisdom, and thanks, we think. But the truth is that more than one-third of all the psalms either are psalms of lament or include lament. Some are individual expressions of lament while others express the lament of a community.

Psalm 88 is perhaps the heaviest and darkest of all the lament psalms. Whereas most laments sooner or later reach some expression of trust, this psalm ends with darkness.

Imagine a believer saying with the psalmist:

> LORD, you are the God who saves me; day and
> night I cry out to you. May my prayer come before
> you; turn your ear to my cry. I am overwhelmed
> with troubles and my life draws near to death. . . .
> Your wrath lies heavily on me; you overwhelmed
> me with all your waves. . . . Why, LORD, do you re-
> ject me and hide your face from me? (Psalm 88:
> 1-3, 7, 14)

A parishioner and very dear friend of mine taught me to look carefully at this psalm. He was thirty-seven years old, the father of three young children, a model teacher, and a courageous Christian man. But he had pancreatic cancer, and in spite of the best medical care he lived less than five months. During the last month of his life, the pain became virtually unbearable, particularly during the hours of the night. I went to see him frequently, and we would have rich conversations and devotions together.

During one of those visits he surprised me by asking what I thought about Psalm 88. He said, "I've read it over and over because it matches so closely what I am experiencing when I lie with pain all night." And then he asked, "Does it bother you that there is no hope in this psalm? It's a cry in anguish and pain all the way through . . . right to the last word. Other laments end with an expression of some form of trust. This one doesn't." He said, "That's how I feel at night. The pain is so unrelenting I can think of nothing else. And somehow I need to get out of that. How do I do it?"

We had one of those deep conversations that can occur between best friends in the toughest of times when they are free to completely open their hearts to one another. He took me into the darkness of those frightful nighttime hours when pain would not let go. I knew that he was a believer who was safe in the love of Christ. He knew it too. So I read the powerful promises of Romans 8 to him and re-assured him that those promises are all true even in that unrelent-ing darkness when he can't feel any of it. I encouraged him to have someone read Romans 8 each evening, and we also arranged to have some recorded music of favorite hymns playing quietly all night. The promises and the hymns could not reverse the pain, but they did prop his faith enough to endure the painful darkness.

Although my friend's body was tormented with pain so that he could hardly think about anything else, God's spoken and sung Word enabled his spirit to hold on to God.

Reflecting on God's Word

Psalm 13
Habakkuk 1:1-14
Romans 8

For Further Reflection

1. How do you feel about expressing a lament—a cry, complaint, or even argument—to God? Do these expressions come from a lack of faith?

2. Examine Psalm 88 again. It's very dark. Compare it with some other laments, such as Psalm 10, 42-43, and 94. How is Psalm 88 different?

3. Should we be free to express lament to our family and friends? Should our worship in church include lament?

10. A Hoax?

Some time ago a family in Colorado was convicted of staging a hoax on the American public. They claimed that their six-year-old son was in a hot air balloon that had inadvertently taken to the air and was traveling rapidly at a high altitude. Perhaps you remember the story. Planes and helicopters were dispatched to follow the balloon's flight. TV cameras converged on the anticipated landing site as the balloon began to descend. TV screens carried the story as the American public sat on the edge of their chairs wondering what would happen to this poor frightened little boy. As it turned out, the little fellow was not on the balloon. He was hiding in the attic of their garage. It was a hoax.

A hoax is a deliberate attempt to deceive other people in the hopes of achieving a certain goal.

At times I've asked myself whether the Christian faith could be a hoax. It was a disturbing and painful question for me—so painful that I never felt free to talk to anyone else about it. It just rolled around inside me. And the more it rolled around the cloudier my life became.

I was about to make my profession of faith. I was intending to prepare for a lifetime of preaching that faith. And even after I began my ministry the question still rolled around at times.

What if this is all a hoax? What if I get to the end and find out I was sincerely mistaken? What if my parents, without realizing it, had instructed me to believe something that isn't true? What if their parents—and the generations before them—had all made the same mistake? How could I be sure?

Several waves of such doubts rolled over me. Sometimes those questions just nagged at me, but other times they tried to strangle me. What a terrible thing it would be to make a lifetime commitment to something that might be a hoax! Even more terrible was the prospect of thinking that I could be preaching and perpetuating a hoax! No wonder the clouds got heavy at times. I should have talked to someone about it but I didn't dare.

One day the clouds lifted for me. And they never came back.

It happened when I was preparing a sermon, of all things! It was a sermon on 1 Corinthians 15. As I worked my way through all the issues Paul was raising, I tried to follow his very logical train of thought. If Christ has not been raised from the dead, then (1) my preaching is useless, (2) my faith is useless, (3) we are all false witnesses about God, (4) we are still in our sins, and (5) all those who died in faith are lost (verse 12-19).

The clouds lifted when I read the first word of 1 Corinthians 15:20: *But.*

The Holy Spirit used that beautiful, comforting, powerful word to lift the clouds and make sure they never came back.

The one thing that could completely destroy the Christian faith would be to discover that Christ is still in that tomb in Palestine. And the one fact that forever establishes the validity and truth of the Christian faith is Christ's resurrection. All other religions have masters and teachers who died and are still dead. Not Christianity. Our leader died and rose again. He actually, physically, bodily came out of the tomb—a historical fact that has been documented and verified by all his post-resurrection appearances. Christ is alive forevermore and thereby establishes the veracity of our faith.

Clouds be gone! Jesus arose!

Reflecting on God's Word

Psalm 16
Matthew 28:1-10
Revelation 1:4-20

For Further Reflection

1. Have you ever felt the clouds of doubt and worry that the Christian faith might be a hoax? When? Are the clouds still present for you?

2. Read 1 Corinthians 15 and write down all the things we would lose if Christ never came out of the tomb.

3. Now read 1 Corinthians 15:1-8. Why do you suppose Paul includes this? Why did Christ remain on earth for forty days after his resurrection, and what did he do during those days?

Healthy Habits

Healthy Habits

The whole idea of habits has taken a bum rap lately. Words like *habit, routine, ritual,* and *discipline* make many people feel like they've just been punched in the stomach. "What good is an empty habit?" they ask, assuming that *empty* and *habit* are synonyms.

Yet my life is built around habits. I get up at about the same time every morning and follow the same ritual—shower, shave, dress, breakfast, and then my quiet time. I leave about the same time for the office, taking the same route each time. I eat lunch about the same time every day. I get my hair cut every five weeks—even as it slowly disappears! I read the newspaper each evening, watch the news, and catch a little shut-eye. I take my walk every evening. I go to church every Sunday.

That may sound boring, but it's really not at all. The regularity and rhythm of such actions give my life safety, security, and comfort. I embrace these habits because they enhance the quality of my life.

Some folks seem to think that the only meaningful actions in life are those we eagerly and consciously decide to do. We do them because we want to, because they attract us, because we feel like it. Anything else is relegated to a lower category of behavior. Those actions are routine, less enjoyable, less significant, even machine-like.

These days, the daily habits that shape my life are predictable and routine. I put very little conscious effort into them . . . I just do them. But long ago I chose every one of those habits. Behind each is the conviction that this is such a valuable thing to do that I want to build it into the fabric and rhythm of my daily life.

The habits of my life reflect more than self-discipline. I have searched, evaluated, and discovered the kinds of actions that help build a healthy, productive, enjoyable, and comfortable life. Putting these practices into place on a regular basis is part of my discipleship—that is, being the kind of disciple my Lord and Savior wants me to be.

Habits make my life more secure because I know I'll be using my time wisely. They protect me from the kind of undisciplined living that leaves behind unfinished tasks, wasted time, poor health, and frazzled relationships.

The kind of habits we develop can shape our lives for good or ill. We'll talk about some healthy habits in this section, but there are many more. Which ones will you include in your life?

1. Observation

People who were born blind have never been able to see what the world around us looks like. But those who lose their eyesight later in life can remember what things look like and can draw on those memories.

One of my parishioners lost his eyesight in a truck accident as a young man. After he and his wife had arrived home from a trip to Florida, he described the beauty of the mountains along the way. His wife had given him commentary as they traveled, and he matched it with his memory. "Wow," he said, "you should have seen how beautiful the Smokies were!"

The world around us is a beautiful sight to behold.

I find that I've developed a very keen sense of sight—maybe because I was afraid at several points that my life would end prematurely. I look around and I actually see! That's more than a lot of folks. I feel sorry for people who can see but don't.

I watch the birds flit back and forth from my feeder. I watch the sun turn the horizon in the east into a blazing fire and in the west into a panorama of oranges, reds, and yellows. I watch the clouds roll by. I see the green of a hummingbird, the red of a cardinal, the yellow of a goldfinch, and the gray of a junco. I notice some insects almost too tiny to observe and squirrels jumping from one branch to another without falling.

In the spring I watch trees green up and new flowers pop their heads above the ground. I watch the hostas in my garden unfurl leaves that are umbrellas for all the little creatures that live beneath them. I prune my roses so they can grow even better. I mow my lawn and wonder how it is that little blades of grass can grow back so quickly. I take my walk at night and notice the configuration of the stars and wonder about the light-years between there and here. Over the years my family and I have enjoyed camping trips not just because it was a chance to get away but because it taught us to see.

So I can imagine the thrill David was feeling when the sheep were bedded down and he lay on his back on the hillside looking up and said, "When I consider your heavens, the work of your fingers, the moon and the stars, which you have set in place . . ." (Psalm 8:3). I can't help but wonder if he had a big lump in his throat when he said that.

David kept his eyes wide open to the wonders of creation, and he heard God's voice speaking through them: "The heavens declare the glory of God; the skies proclaim the work of his hands. Day after day they pour forth speech; night after night they display knowledge" (Psalm 19:1-2).

Seeing and hearing go together. I see best when I hear creation's wordless message about the creative hand of God.

So one of my habits each day is to see. From the first glimpse of daylight to the creatures that fly and crawl, from the sky above and the earth beneath, the blowing leaves, the setting sun, the clouds that float by, and the stars that sparkle. What a sight! What a creation!

What a Creator!

Reflecting on God's Word

Genesis 1
Job 38-41
Psalm 104

For Further Reflection

1. Read Psalm 8 again. What conclusions did David draw about himself and about God after he had been out star-gazing for a while?

2. Read Job 38-41. What was God was trying to communicate to Job in these chapters?

3. Think of a road trip or vacation you took or your recent drive to work. What did you see in nature that spoke to you about God? What did it say?

2. Receiving

The habit we'll reflect on today is the act of "receiving."

Maybe that sounds far too passive to you. Of course we receive, you may be thinking. All the time. And in receiving we do nothing but sit back and let come what comes.

But the kind of receiving I'm thinking of is much more intentional and active. It involves reaching out and taking. It involves noticing the value of what we take, realizing the gift character of what we receive, welcoming it, and giving thanks for it.

This kind of active receiving can be a healthy antidote to what may be a major sin of middle-class Christians—passively receiving everything with hardly a thought of gratitude. Too often we live with a sense of entitlement instead of gratitude.

Church signs tend to catch my eye as I drive. Some are inane and corny. Others make me think. The other day I passed one that stirred my determination to actively receive. It said, "God owes us nothing— but gives us everything." That's right on! And it cultivates an attitude that can stir up some very healthy humility in our hearts.

That sign reminded me of Paul's rhetorical question to the Corinthian Christians as he attempted to teach them to set aside their pride and learn humility: "What do you have that you did not receive?" (1 Corinthians 4:7). Paul's focus is on both God's generosity and our undeserved wealth.

> All things are yours, whether Paul or Apollos or Cephas or the world or life or death or the present or the future—all are yours, and you are of Christ, and Christ is of God (1 Corinthians 3:21-23).

So I'm suggesting that we begin each day quietly noticing and intentionally reaching out to gratefully receive all the good gifts God has for us this day. Try to actively receive in such a way that your heart reaches in thankfulness to the Giver.

- Receive the day as it dawns—morning light, air to breathe, and the promise of activity and relationships that will fill the day.

- Receive the provisions that come—a home, breakfast, clothes to wear, freedom, a safe neighborhood, work to do, and protective care.
- Receive the creation around you—the sunrise, the rain, changing seasons, colorful flowers, darting birds, trees for shade, rivers, hills, and gardens.
- Receive the people who are given to you—spouse, family, special friends, neighbors, and coworkers.
- Receive the promises of God that are new every morning—"I will keep you, bless you, hold you, forgive you, and always walk with you."
- Receive the richness of the new life in Christ—adoption into God's family, union with him, grace for pardon, big purposes for which to live, and hope for eternity.

Those of us who have come near to losing our lives to some dread disease or perhaps in some accident find it easier to notice all these, to actively reach out and receive them and lift our hearts with quick "Thanks, God!" exclamations all day long.

But all of us can choose to develop the habit of receiving God's gifts with a thousand thanks daily.

Reflecting on God's Word

Deuteronomy 8:6-20
Psalm 103
Luke 17:11-19

For Further Reflection

1. How did you react to the suggestion that a major sin of middle-class Christians is "passively receiving everything with hardly a thought of gratitude"? What evidence can you find to support that in your own life and the life of others?

2. Identify and reflect on a few experiences in your life that have led you to notice and appreciate certain gifts more than ever.

3. Resolve that, starting today, you will begin to send up thanks-prayers to God all day. Do it every time you notice another of God's gifts to you.

3. Affirm Life

Life has become very precious to me. I value life more today than I have at any other time. Maybe that's because I'm older now, and hopefully I've acquired some seasoning through the years. Maybe it comes from the privilege of watching my children and grandchildren live and grow. But I can't escape the awareness that it has also come from my narrow escapes and the possibility of losing my life to cancer those three times.

Certain events permanently shape our perspective on things. Captain Chesley "Sully" Sullenberger, the pilot who put his plane down in the Hudson River in January 2009, wrote a book called *Highest Duty*. In it he explained how certain events early in life shaped him for his career. He tells of the time when he was thirteen years old in 1964 and the evening news carried a story about the attack on Kitty Genovese of Queens, New York. Genovese was sexually assaulted and stabbed to death outside her apartment. He was shocked to hear that folks who'd heard her cries for help ignored them. No one responded; no one called the police. "Sully" made a pledge to himself that he would always "show up for life"—and abandon no one. His life illustrates a pattern of such a commitment—culminating in the courage that led him to land his disabled aircraft in the Hudson River, saving all the passengers and crew.

Affirming life is a good habit for all of us. In his devotional book *Bread for the Journey,* Henri Nouwen calls us to "do everything possible to show our friends that, though their lives may be short, they are of infinite value."

For us it begins with the conviction that God has created us in his own image. We build our living on God's words in the very first chapter of Genesis: "So God created human beings in his own image, in the image of God he created them; male and female he created them" (1:27).

And we resonate with David's exclamation "I praise you because I am fearfully and wonderfully made; your works are wonderful, I know that full well" (Psalm 139:14).

Those truths not only enable us to see ourselves as sacred, valuable, and created in the image of God, but to see others that way too. We learn the habit of seeing all others that way—a newborn baby, a misbehaving child, an adolescent, a businesswoman, a busy father, a fragile senior. Those who are healthy or obese or disabled or tall or short, those who are from our own race or from another. Those who are likable and those who are not. Though there are many differences among us, all people have this in common: they are alive. They possess the life God has given them, and they deserve to be treated with respect and care.

The habit of "showing up for life," as Sullenberg put it, enables us to accept others whom we wouldn't otherwise accept, to be kind and compassionate to everyone in need, to reach out and serve them instead of ignoring them, to exercise care that will protect others, even those we may not know.

Cultivating the habit of affirming life will make our homes, communities, churches, and society a healthier and much safer place for all.

To life!

Reflecting on God's Word

Exodus 1:8-22
Luke 10:25-37
James 2:1-13

For Further Reflection

1. Of the three passages above, cite the instances in which participants in the story refused to "show up for life" and thereby hurt others. Notice how, in the same story, there were others who protected and valued the lives of others.

2. Recall an instance in which you allowed prejudice to shape your reactions to someone. How might that have hurt that person? What should you have done?

3. What could you do today that would intentionally communicate to others that, no matter who they are, you value them as a human being?

4. Hearing

"**A**re you listening to me?" My mother often said that to me when I was a child. She knew I could hear; she just wasn't sure I was paying attention to what she was saying. Only the things I wanted to hear would get through.

The Bible has a lot to say about hearing and listening. Speaking on God's behalf, Isaiah said to the people of Israel, "Give ear and come to me; listen that you may live" (Isaiah 55:3).

Jesus often said, "Whoever has ears, let them hear" (Matthew 11:15). To illustrate the importance of hearing and listening, he told a parable about four soils called "The Parable of the Sower." You can read it in Matthew, Mark, and Luke.

In the book of Revelation, John's letters to the seven churches all end with the same charge: "Whoever has ears, let them hear what the Spirit says to the churches" (Revelation 2 and 3).

There's so much to listen to! I mean things that are really worthwhile. We have the voice of our conscience, which speaks to us constantly—but encounters a lot of interference. We have the voices of the people God has placed in our lives to lead us—but it's easy to ignore what our parents, friends, counselors, teachers, and pastors say. We have the voice of the Spirit who nudges our hearts in so many ways—but we miss so many of the Spirit's promptings. Above all, we have the voice of God directly from his Word—but we find it easier to read other things.

Our ability to hear the big things in life has fallen on hard times. We seem to hear so much but listen so little. Good listening takes protection from interference and clear uncluttered channels. It takes times of silence. But the noise level in our lives is so high that good listening is impossible.

Silence can be scary. It can make us very uncomfortable. So we have a whole range of gadgets to protect us from silence—radio, TV, iPods, and other noisemakers all distract us from the possibility of quiet.

Maybe God sometimes places experiences in our lives that force us to be quiet so we can hear better. If you've been in the hospital for more than a day or two, you know what I mean. If you've had to step aside from the busyness of life to convalesce for a while, you know that silence can make hearing much easier.

I need the healthy habit of hearing and listening to God. So I've needed my times of sickness. I've needed times when the radio and TV are turned off, times when I just drive and think, times when I work in my yard with my ears wide open in the silence. Above all I need times to sit in my favorite chair with my Bible on my lap, times of listening to God's Word.

"Whoever has ears, let them hear," said Jesus. He was talking to us too.

Reflecting on God's Word

Genesis 3:1-13
Matthew 13:10-17
Romans 10:14-17

For Further Reflection

1. Find a place where you can be alone and sit quietly for five minutes. Then ask yourself how that felt, what you thought of, and what you heard.

2. How do you make quiet space in your life for regular devotions? How might you want to change your practice? What kinds of passages do you read from the Bible?

3. How does the church you attend provide times of silence in the service to aid your reflection and listening? What enables you to listen well to a sermon?

5. Reflection

When our three boys were young, we spent every summer vacation camping together. We enjoyed the leisure time together, treasured the outdoors, and became acquainted with different regions of the country.

Camping vacations always create special memories. Some of the best of our family memories center on storytelling time when the boys would crawl into their sleeping bags for a "Clem story." Every evening the task of telling a Clem story was mine. Clem was a fictitious character—we have no idea where he came from—but he was an integral part of our family vacations year after year. Every night as the boys snuggled down into their sleeping bags, they'd say, "Tell us about Clem." So I did.

"Once upon a time there was a blond little boy by the name of Clem . . ." I'd begin. The same way every evening. I'd tell about all the events of Clem's day—who he met, what he did, where he went, how he felt, what made him happy, what made him sad . . . everything I could think of. By some strange coincidence, the events of Clem's day were always identical to what our day had been like. What Clem did was exactly what we had done. When we went hiking, Clem did too. When we saw a waterfall, so did Clem. When we defeated someone in Rummy, so did Clem.

When the boys were very young they found it very ironic that Clem did the same things we had done and went the same places we had gone. But gradually it dawned on them that they were Clem! The bedtime story became a time to look back on the day and relive it through Clem's adventures. Today those boys are grown men, and they still talk about Clem stories from time to time.

What the boys didn't realize at the time was that they were being taught a highly valuable habit for living life well: the art of reflecting on what we do, why we do it, and how we feel about it. Reflection and review leads to thoughtful living.

Those who do that kind of reflection are healthier for it. The Bible is full of examples of people who engage in reflection. David was doing it when he said to God, "May these words of my mouth and this meditation of my heart be pleasing in your sight, Lord, my Rock and my Redeemer" (Psalm 19:14). And after the angel visited with the amazing news that Mary would be the mother of the Savior, Luke tells us that she "treasured up all these things and pondered them in her heart" (Luke 2:19).

Some of us write in diaries or journals, giving us the opportunity to reflect on the events, experiences, and feelings of the day. Some may just use a quiet time at the end of the day to muse over the day's happenings. In some marriages and families, a quiet conversation at the end of the day serves this purpose. Whatever method we use, it's a time to get off the fast track, shut down the noise, and enter into a time of contemplation. Doing that helps us resist the tendency to move on to the next day without first thinking through what this day involved. It allows us to go through our day with a desire to learn from it, to recognize where God's voice was coming through, and to give thanks for people, events, and circumstances that God has given us.

If you develop the healthy habit of reflection, you'll be better able to recognize God's gifts during the day. You'll be more conscious of the way God has used you. And maybe you'll even notice some missed opportunities along the way.

Reflecting on God's Word

Deuteronomy 5:12-15
Psalm 105
Philippians 4:8-9

For Further Reflection

1. If you regularly keep a diary or write in a journal, read back through some of the entries and try to identify how God has led you. If not, try doing so for a month. Each day, write a few short sentences about what happened and how you felt about it.

2. What memories and practices are you leaving with your children or your friends' children that can help them live a life that includes examination and reflection?

3. As you reflect on the pattern of your life over the past two or three years, what do you see and how do you feel about it?

6. Cleansing

Cleanliness is good for our health, I'm told. So I wash my face every day. I wash my hands many times each day. I shower on a daily basis. I always seem to feel better when I feel clean—except when I'm out working in my yard and flowers and getting "dirty" feels just right.

Germs are all around: on telephones, faucets, keyboards, doorknobs, our desks at work. If you ever get a chance to look at some of these germs under a microscope, you'll understand why I wash so often!

But there's another kind of "dirt" I have to cleanse away on a regular basis—the sins I am guilty of and the temptations I deal with. They cling to me as vigorously as the germs on my faucet handle. So I need to get rid of them regularly.

Many Christians don't like to talk about their sins. They find confessing sins a rather distasteful experience, something to put behind them. And so their prayers don't include much confession. They'd rather not be called to confession of their sins in worship either. They believe their sins are all forgiven and want to move forward from there.

But think about this. My home is a nice, comfortable, clean place to be. Even though we love it, something happens at my home so regularly that it needs daily attention. Dirt collects, so we have to vacuum and dust the place. Garbage accumulates, so we have to take it out nearly every day.

In his book *Beyond Doubt,* Cornelius Plantinga Jr. says confessing sins is like taking the garbage out. You can ignore it, you can say you don't have it—but after a while such behavior will make for a very unhealthy home. So you take out the garbage on a regular basis.

Similarly, Christians need the healthy habit of regularly confessing their sins. They don't do that because Christ hasn't forgiven them. They know that Jesus' death on the cross and his resurrection takes care of all their sins—past, present, and future. In his sight we are "clean" all the time, as far as our guilt is concerned. But to live in that assurance we need to get rid of all the "germs" around. That makes us healthier.

The apostle John counseled believers to "take out the garbage" regularly: "If we claim to be without sin, we deceive ourselves and the truth is not in us. If we confess our sins, he is faithful and just and will forgive us our sins and purify us from all unrighteousness" (1 John 1:8-9).

I'm a healthier person when I'm washed clean. My morning shower gets me ready for the day. And I'm a healthier person when I've brought my sins to God for cleansing. Confessing my sins helps me to walk in the light of the deep assurance he has for me. The good news of the gospel is that I never have to wonder whether it's safe or not to confess to him.

Jesus is always a safe place. He's my Savior!

◎ Reflecting on God's Word

Psalm 32
Romans 8:1
1 John 2:1-2

◎ For Further Reflection

1. How would you answer those who say that since they have been forgiven by Christ, there is no need to confess their sins anymore?

2. Sometimes there are specific and "major" sins we need to confess; sometimes those sins are less obvious. Should both kinds be confessed just as faithfully?

3. Write down three pointed promises from the Bible that give you assurance of your forgiveness. Then post them in a prominent place where you will see them daily.

7. Commit the Day

Organized and structured people—like me—tend to plan their days carefully, stick to a schedule, and live with a "to do" list. I do that because it fits my personality well and because it helps me to be more efficient and productive. It helps me to avoid the empty feeling at the end the day that I have nothing to show for it.

But it means I live with the baffling tension between planning a day's schedule and allowing people (and God) to bring interruptions that often reroute the day—or at least part of it. Between planning carefully and holding the plan loosely. Between believing that I am in charge of my own schedule and submitting my schedule to God, who is the ultimate planner.

The life of a pastor involves constantly dealing with what we think of as interruptions. A single knock on the door, a single phone call can cause a schedule to evaporate. When is something a genuine interruption, and when is it an unscheduled appointment planned by God? That's an issue pastors deal with—and so do parents, business people, and probably everyone else too.

One of the problems I've had to face in my tendency to schedule my days is that there might be a subtle form of idolatry creeping in. Is it possible that I think I'm the ultimate planner, and my scheduled plans are inviolable? Sometimes I have wondered whether I've put myself and my plans in the place where only God belongs.

The apostle James saw this happening around him: "Now listen, you who say, 'Today or tomorrow we will go to this or that city, spend a year there, carry on business and make money.' Why, you do not even know what will happen tomorrow. . . . Instead, you ought to say, 'If it is the Lord's will, we will live and do this or that.' As it is, you boast in your arrogant schemes. All such boasting is evil" (James 4:13-16).

Eventually, through the years, we learn that lesson. Our minds finally grasp the fact that we are not the final determiner of our days (how many we have) and our schedules (what goes into those days).

But we also learn James's lesson through the sudden changes that come upon us unexpectedly. With no advance warning at all our lives can be rerouted, and everything we had planned becomes negotiable. I learned that the hard way when I was scheduled for my first surgery. Trying to negotiate with the doctor on when to schedule the surgery, I pointed out the commitments I had for just about every day he suggested. Finally he interrupted and said, "We'll do it Tuesday, and you must rearrange your schedule."

That experience taught me that a vital healthy habit for each day is to commit the day and its plans to the Lord, who supervises them all.

My morning prayer often includes something like the following:

> Lord, thanks so much for the day you've given. I have things to do and plans that I've made. Help me to discern what you have in mind for me today, to willingly accept the changes that your plans require, and to make the most of the gift of this day.

Committing each new day to the Lord as it begins is an act of faith.

Reflecting on God's Word

Psalm 39
Matthew 6:25-34
Ephesians 5:15-20

For Further Reflection

1. Remind yourself of an occasion or two in recent years when God's plans have significantly changed or interrupted your plans. How did you handle that?

2. In what ways can it be idolatry to hold on too tightly to the plans that we make for ourselves?

3. A generation ago many Christians included the initials "DV"—*deo volente,* which means "God willing"—to make announcements about their plans. We rarely hear that today. In what ways could we retrieve that awareness?

8. Body Care

There was a time when I was guilty of abusing my body—or at least not caring for it as thoughtfully as God expected of me. During my high school and college years I didn't get enough sleep or exercise. My diet was poor and I smoked cigarettes. Looking back, I can see that some of those abuses led to some of my early health problems.

One day, a doctor in a small town hospital sat down on the foot of my bed to explain some things about my bleeding ulcer. "Look," he said, "your body is like a house. Our houses are nice places and they will serve us for a long time . . ." and here he deliberately paused, "*if* (and his pointed finger found me in its cross-hairs) we take care of it! Take care of your body, and it will last you a long time. But if you abuse it, you will find that it breaks down easily."

This was the wake-up call I needed. The doctor raised issues that I had not learned well enough. Among other things, a productive life is built on adequate care of our physical bodies.

Maybe you're wondering why, if I learned to care for my body, I've had three bouts with two different strains of cancer. Shouldn't I have been able to avoid those if I cared well for my health?

But here's how I see it—we are all surrounded by the risk of diseases of all sorts. Our bodies have a built-in immune system that works 24/7 to protect us. Threats are everywhere—within us and around us. We care for our bodies not just to avoid getting diseases but so that we can fight a good fight against them when they do attack us.

Although taking care of my body didn't prevent me from dealing with cancer three times, it equipped me to fight the disease. First, two of my three encounters with cancer were detected at a very early stage during a routine physical examination when there were no symptoms at all. If not for those annual exams, perhaps the disease would have advanced too far before it was detected. In all three encounters with cancer, I recovered well from the surgeries and was able to tolerate the radiation treatments. It has now been twenty years since my third diagnosis, and I am in superb health, given my age. Caring for "my house" has required some big repairs, but it continues to serve me well.

Good body care is a healthy habit for our own benefit. But there's an even higher motive for it. Scripture teaches that God created us in our mother's womb (Psalm 139). Our bodies belong to God, and we owe it to God to care for it well. Here are just a few examples of what the Bible has to say with respect to our bodies:

- "Offer your bodies as a living sacrifice, holy and pleasing to God . . ." (Romans 12:2).
- "Your bodies are temples of the Holy Spirit, who is in you, whom you have received from God" (1 Corinthians 6:19).
- At the final resurrection God ". . . will transform our lowly bodies so that they will be like his glorious body" (Philippians 3:21).

If God has carefully crafted these bodies for us, if our bodies are the "homes" in which we live, then surely proper care, nutrition, rest, exercise, and medical care are part of our obedience to God.

Make it a habit to care for your physical body, God's gift to you.

Reflecting on God's Word

Genesis 2:4-9
Luke 5:12-16
James 5:13-16

For Further Reflection

1. Reflect on your attention to the care of your body. For some folks it may be too much; for others too little. How would you evaluate your balance between those two?

2. Which of the major areas of care—nutrition, sleep, exercise, medical attention—are in need of some change in order to achieve a good balance?

3. At times Christians have felt awkward talking about the importance of our bodies as part of our Christian life. They have downplayed the importance of the body in favor of "the soul." What are some reasons for the importance and value of our physical body?

9. Leisure

Leisure, rest, and play are gifts from God for us to enjoy. That's hard for us to learn. The balance God intends for our lives often seems very difficult to discover.

That's because we are often caught between two opposing viewpoints. On the one hand our work ethic exalts the value of working hard. It easily leads us to conclude that if we are not working hard we have less value and dignity. On the other hand the middle-class culture many of us are part of does just the opposite by exalting play, leisure, and pleasure. We're told that we owe it to ourselves to take a big vacation, retire early, and enjoy as much pleasure as possible. So which is it? And how can we ever hope to find a balance between the two?

Like you, I've lived my whole life in the middle of those conflicting pressures. I never had a problem with learning the habit of work. It was the habit of leisure that took more intentionality.

Several factors became my counselors. My sons taught me that although my vocation required a great deal of time and effort, spending time with them was more important in the long run than work. Periods of time when I became exhausted from intense work led a friend to remind me that the fourth commandment about a Sabbath was meant for pastors too. And then I read a book by Tim Hansel called *When I Relax I Feel Guilty* that pinpointed the exact problem I was dealing with.

Gradually I began to understand why God said, "Remember the Sabbath day by keeping it holy. . . . For in six days the LORD made the heavens and the earth, the sea, and all that is in them, but he rested on the seventh day. Therefore the LORD blessed the Sabbath day and made it holy" (Exodus 20:8, 11).

And because Jesus' disciples were so busy with their ministry, Jesus said to them, "'Come with me by yourselves to a quiet place and get some rest.' So they went away by themselves in a boat to a solitary place" (Mark 6:31-32).

A healthy rhythm in life calls for habituated leisure—neither all work nor all leisure. Therefore our life will be best balanced when our work is punctuated with times of leisure. I've found five areas of including leisure in my life.

Holy Sabbath. The Lord's Day was made holy by God himself. It's not just a day to set work aside but to worship, spend time with loved ones, and center ourselves again in the work of God.

Rest and sleep. With good purpose God planned that each day should include "evening and morning." We need time to set our work aside, rest our mind, and refresh our body. These cannot be ignored without major consequences.

Vacation. When we get away and leave our stress behind, we have opportunities to see God's creation, enjoy relationships, and be renewed.

Laughter. Times of laughter and fun are like mini-vacations that do their own work of renewal. Heavy is the life that is always serious; healthy is the life with a wholesome sense of humor.

Hobbies. When we find enjoyable and creative activities that relieve our stress, we have found an oasis to renew our spirit and mind.

Reflecting on God's Word

Psalm 104:1-23
Ecclesiastes 3:1-13
Luke 5:15-16

For Further Reflection

1. Evaluate the balance between work and leisure in your life. Do you work too much or too little? How do you make sure the people in your life receive the attention from you they need?

2. How do you feel when you relax? Guilty? Renewed? What difference might it make to understand that leisure is necessary for healthy living?

3. Which of the five ways listed above are most important to you? Which others would you add?

10. Spending

Occasionally I'll calculate how much money passes through my hands and my checkbook in a month's time. Stopping to take note of how much it is usually stirs in me a sense of amazement at the abundance in my life and also a huge sense of responsibility to manage it well.

I've seen too many people whose lives have been ruined because they've allowed their money to run away with them. I've seen too many people who have created a shamble of things because of poor management. And I've seen too many noble causes—within the church and outside of it—that have gone wanting because others were too tight-fisted to support it. For all these reasons I have come to realize that the management of our checkbook is a strategic habit in the well-ordered Christian life.

I remember the days when we had to manage very carefully because our family expenses were high and our income was low. Every dollar had to be accounted for or we would never meet our obligations. Now that our children are grown, our expenses are lower, and we are more affluent, we must still carefully account for everything. Doing so is part of our obedience to Christ.

Our society loves "bigger barns," and our appetite for material success seems almost unquenchable. The Bible makes it clear that there are two methods to achieve "bigger barns." One method is to work hard, manage carefully, and keep adding. It's the "I can do it" approach that marks many of us. In one of his parables, Jesus characterizes such people as a man who planned to tear down his barns and build bigger ones to store his surplus. Then he would say to himself, "Take life easy; eat, drink and be merry" (Luke 12:19). His life was built on the conviction that life consists "in the abundance of possessions" (Luke 12:15).

But long before Jesus told that parable, God had instructed his people that there is a better way to fill barns. The prophet Malachi warned the people of Israel against robbing God by refusing to be generous. He instructed them on how to manage their spending:

Bring the whole tithe into the storehouse, that there may be food in my house. Test me in this . . . and see if I will not throw open the floodgates of heaven and pour out so much blessing that there will not be room enough to store it (Malachi 3:10).

There you have two approaches. Fill your barns by working hard. Accumulate possessions, assuming that they determine the value of your life. Or take what God provides, be generous with it, and be amazed at God's blessings.

No Christian can live well without the habit of supervised spending. Our checkbooks show a lot about our spiritual health; our spending and giving reveal our value system. And our value system reveals our allegiance to Christ and his kingdom.

Each of us must faithfully consider how much we will give to our local church and to other worthy causes. Each of us must decide which causes dear to our heart will be the benefactors of our generosity. Each of us must decide whether we will tithe or more from all that God gives us. Each of us must decide how much to save.

We need to cultivate the habit of holding loosely to what we earn, knowing that the value of our life does not consist of the abundance of what we possess.

It's the habit of discerning how to spend wisely.

Reflecting on God's Word

Proverbs 3:9-10
Luke 16:1-13
2 Corinthians 9:6-15

For Further Reflection

1. If someone studied your finances for a month or two, what conclusions do you think they would draw about your value system?

2. Do you practice tithing? More than a tithe? Less? How do you make your decisions about that?

3. How do you understand the story from Luke 16 cited above? What does it *not* mean? What is the point of it?

Epilogue

ife is a journey. Some journeys are long; others are short. Some are rather predictable; others unpredictable. Some are very difficult; some not.

I see the richness of my life more clearly now than ever because of my times spent in God's crucible. Through these pages, I have shared some of my richest experiences and also some of my deepest pain. I've tried to help you see that God intends for us to live life to the full.

My aim in sharing my story and my journey is to encourage you in your journey. I have benefitted greatly from being allowed to peek inside the stories of other people's lives as I've lived mine. My hope is the same for you.

There are so many wonders for us to see and enjoy. God spreads many gifts and provisions before us every day, so receive them with thanks. Our lives and times are uncertain in many ways, but we can learn to trust God lovingly. Each one of the years we're given is filled with potential, so let's use them wisely.

When we sink our roots deeply into the riches of God's love and the security of God's promises we find ourselves equipped to live well . . . no matter what the journey holds.